CHOICES

Never-Ending Dilemmas in Everyday Life

by

Arthur Asa Berger

San Francisco State University

Illustrated by the Author

Series in Sociology

VERNON PRESS

In the Americas:
Vernon Press
1000 N West Street, Suite 1200,
Wilmington, Delaware 19801
United States

In the rest of the world:
Vernon Press
C/Sancti Espiritu 17,
Malaga, 29006
Spain

Series in Sociology

Library of Congress Control Number: 2023947656

ISBN: 978-1-64889-796-2

Illustrated with drawings and photographs by the author.

Cover design by Vernon Press. Cover image by Arthur Asa Berger.

Table of Contents

Dedication   vii

Epigraph   ix

Foreword   xi
Bob Batchelor

Preface   xv

Acknowledgments   xvii

List of Illustrations   xix

List of Tables   xxi

Takeways   xxiii

PART ONE: THEORIES   1

Chapter 1   **The Social-Anthropology of Choice**   3

Chapter 2   **Marxism and Choices**   7

Chapter 3   **Espresso Machine Aficionados: A Case Study**   11

Chapter 4   **The Sociology of Choice**   21

Chapter 5   **The Semiotics of Choice**   35

Chapter 6   **Choice and the Psyche**   45

PART TWO: APPLICATIONS   55

Chapter 7   **Choosing a Partner**   57

Chapter 8   **Work**   63

Chapter 9   **Housing**   71

Chapter 10   **Ocean Cruising Tourism**   75

Chapter 11   **Gender Choice**   85

Chapter 12   **Coda**   91

Glossary   99

References   119

About the Author   123

Index of Names   125

Index of Topics   127

Arthur Asa Berger has done it again. He has written a book that is a philosophical treatise in ontology, a semiotic analysis of the objects and events of everyday life, and a practical guide to the meaning and logic of our unconscious activities, seamlessly uniting all these threads into a masterpiece of purveyance of life's meaning. And he does all this in user-friendly language, explaining and practically illustrating profound ideas from philosophy, semiotics, and cultural analysis in an enjoyable way, as well as critiquing them when they need to be critiqued, making the book truly a great "read."

Marcel Danesi
Professor Emeritus, Anthropology
University of Toronto

Drawing from influential theories like semiotics, this invaluable book delves into the power and mechanism of choices we make. It offers practical insights into decision-making, shedding light on the pivotal role of choice in our society, culture, and personal lives, where some choices we make shape our destinies.

Dr. Yoshiko Okuyama
Professor, Japanese
Department of Languages
University of Hawaii at Hilo

Professor Berger has an excellent knowledge of the most important studies in this field and uses them extensively in his book.
He explores the phenomenon of "choice" from different perspectives -semiotic, psychoanalytic, sociological, political, etc. [and] analyses these standpoints with numerous concrete examples.
The style of the book is quite attractive. Professor Berger adheres to readability requirements and writes with a wonderful sense of humour.
[He] is also an inpired cartoonist who illustrated the book with many cartoons. This is also good with regard to the book's attractiveness and readability.
[He] has also written a glossary of key terms relating to the main topics of the book.
[...] the book is a serious scientific achievement [and] very readable [...]

Dr. Christo Kaftandjiev
Professor, Faculty of Journalism
Sofia University, Bulgaria

Dedication

For Junchao Wang in appreciation of his friendship and his role in introducing my work to Chinese media and communication scholars and students.

Epigraph

I do not at all believe in human freedom in the philosophical sense. Everybody acts not only under external compulsion but also in accordance with inner necessity. Schopenhauer's saying, "**A man can do what he [wants], but not [want] what he [wants]**" has been a very real inspiration to me since my youth; it has been a continual consolation in the face of life's hardships, my own and others', and an unfailing well-spring of tolerance. (Boldface by A.A. Berger)

Edwards' principal reasons *for* theological determinism are God's sovereignty, the principle of sufficient reason (which requires that everything that begins to have a complete cause), the nature of motivation, and God's foreknowledge. The latter two are discussed at length. The argument from motivation depends upon Edwards' identification of willing or choosing with one's strongest inclination or preference. Since choosing just is a prevailing inclination, it is logically impossible to choose in the absence of a prevailing motive. If there is a prevailing motive, however, then the will is necessarily determined by it, for if the will were to choose contrary to a prevailing motive, the agent would have two opposed preponderant inclinations at the same time. All choices, therefore, are necessarily determined.

Stanford Encyclopedia of Philosophy. (n.d.). "Edwards, Jonathan."

Foreword

Bob Batchelor

Arthur Asa Berger is a magician (some would say trickster) whose specialty is making the difficult deceptively easy. He is particularly adept at writing about complex ideas – like the topic at hand – choices. As a matter of fact, if there were a central, foundational thread across all of Berger's work, that defining perspective would be "illumination"…a fancy word for explaining, enlightening, and clarifying.

Or, as he concludes in *Choices: Never Ending Dilemmas in Everyday Life*:

> I hope that this book on choices will have given you some ideas about the role of choices we make in our lives, our society, our culture and our politics (among other things) and that you will be more mindful of the choices you make about both mundane and trivial matters and about significant and life shaping/ life changing choices you make, as well.

The extended quote above leads one to another Berger trick – making the philosophical applicable. As a cultural theorist existing in the "real world" and expecting that readers exist there too (unlike many academic/scholarly writers), he is interested in how they will engage with ideas. Accordingly, Berger asks the reader to "be more mindful" and hopes that his illuminations result in presenting "some ideas" that lead to more informed choices "both mundane and trivial." Isn't this the ultimate goal of the philosopher – to provide the public with ways to navigate their lives?

Let's look a little deeper, though, at the magician behind the words. Berger uses sleight-of-hand (trickster, remember?) to ease the reader's mind, while he not only clarifies the topic, but also provides a mental model for how a person makes choices. In other words, the act of writing and illustrating is in itself a demonstration of choices. (Would any other cultural theorist/philosopher would have the audacity to illustrate their own books as Berger does in his distinct style?) Brilliant!

The other conspicuous choice Berger makes in *Choices* is to use "relatable" (an incredibly twenty-first century word) examples to bring to life the ideas of many of the world's most complex writers and thinkers. For example, he examines Karl Marx's ideas about work, but rather than a regurgitation or recitation, Berger uses it as a springboard to discuss the changing nature of work based on the Covid-19 global pandemic and recent calls for a universal four-day workweek.

As Berger notes, the choices employees (or is it more reasonable to say ex-employees) are making has an enormous consequence to the global economy. "The most important event involving work in recent times was the Covid-19 epidemic," he explains. "It disrupted work arrangements everywhere and has led to new perspectives on work by many people. They found that they liked not having to go to the office every day, avoiding the need to commute, and could do their work at home in a more pleasant (and less dangerous) atmosphere."

Here, the author demonstrates how Marx's thinking endures. Even with the difficult economy, workers are making their own decisions, which is a stark contrast to the historical relationship where the employer/corporation had all the power. In the past, the power relationship titled heavily toward the entity and those in power ultimately determined a person's work status and employability. Today, workers are choosing a different path – instead of opting out, whether it is sliding into a more fluid "gig" economy that enables them to live a different type of lifestyle or dropping from the employment ranks altogether.

The power of Berger's style and analysis is that he is authoritative and engaging, not forcing or bludgeoning the reader with one perspective or way of thinking. Here's the trickster at work again...a writer fluid and conversant with the greatest thinkers in world history, yet introducing the reader to them in a way that is edifying rather than alienating.

What makes Berger so important as a thinker is that he has gladly taken on this role of public educator while existing for most of his life inside the stuffy walls of academe, noted for research that is an inch wide and a mile deep, where the generalist is scorned, along with anything that sniffs of popular culture that is not theory-laden.

We get a glimpse of Berger's own choices in *Choices*, both at the micro- and macro-levels. Again, he is writing the book and using the exercise to demonstrate how a person makes choices. For the reader, then, the application of the author's analysis springs to life. Writ large, Berger explains:

> I had around 40,000 word choices to make, though in many cases, because of the nature of language, once I had chosen certain words, other words followed logically. This means that my choice of words is connected to all kinds of things and is not innocent. When use words, we must assume our listeners or readers know the codes that give them meaning. That means, when I'm writing, I want to make sure that my readers know the codes and can understand what I'm writing, which explains my accessible (as best I can) writing style.

From a sentence-by-sentence perspective, we see a different mode of analysis, one much more pertinent to how people assess information. "If you think of a book as like a trial," Berger says, "The people whose ideas and quotes I offer can be thought of as witnesses for the defense, since my books are, in the final analysis, arguments about a topic that I am making." Most people encounter this same type of analysis in crime dramas on television or film and in the countless thrillers, mysteries, and true crime books published each year. For Berger, he is simply serving up another form of assessment in a way that people are familiar with and can put to use right away.

THE POWER OF *CHOICES*

What I hope readers will gather from this brief essay is that the value of Berger's *Choices* is that I am attempting to model his analysis and style. More importantly, both being a lifelong reader/admirer of his work and engaging with *Choices*, I have made deliberate changes in my own thinking about choice.

For example, Berger's analysis and ideas have led me to double-down on my decision-making as a consumer and creator of culture. After reading *Choices*, I am rethinking how my purchasing options have consequences, including what types of brands I want to support as a buyer. Along these lines, one might ask: Does a specific brand and its leadership align with my feelings about diversity, equity, and inclusion? Or, a reader might question how their seemingly mundane choices ultimately have consequences in relation to the global climate crisis or economic disparities.

Choices is ultimately a testament to Berger's standing as a cultural theorist and writer. In the ever-evolving landscape of ideas, with countless images, impulses, and declarations raining down on us in every conscious moment, Berger guides us as we navigate the complicated tapestry of human expression and societal dynamics.

There are simply few cultural critics who have been able to achieve what he has accomplished or at such a prolific pace. The Library of Congress, for example, lists about 140 books he has written, while sources show that he has been cited more than 25,000 times. As a fellow author, I shudder at the notion that both of these figures are probably underreported.

I count us lucky to live in an "Age of Berger," in which a thinker of his eminent stature has provided readers with a lifetime of work that has helped people understand themselves, as well as their families, communities, and society at large. By every possible definition, Arthur Asa Berger is an intellectual force whose contributions to the realm of cultural theory and the global body of knowledge have left an indelible mark on our understanding of the world around us. Choices indeed!

Bob Batchelor is a cultural historian and biographer. He wrote *Stan Lee: A Life*; *Stan Lee: The Man Behind Marvel, Young Adult Edition*; *Roadhouse Blues: Morrison, the Doors, and the Death Days of the Sixties*; and others looking at contemporary history. His books have won three Independent Book Awards and been translated into a dozen languages. Batchelor's work has appeared in *Time*, *The New York Times*, *PopMatters*, *Cincinnati Enquirer*, and *Los Angeles Times*. He is the creator and host of the podcasts "Tales of the Bourbon King: The Life and True Crimes of George Remus" and "John Updike: American Writer, American Life." He has appeared as an on-air commentator for The National Geographic Channel, *PBS NewsHour*, Wondery, and NPR.

Bob received a doctorate at the University of South Florida. He has taught at universities in Florida, Ohio, and Pennsylvania, as well as Vienna, Austria. Bob lives in North Carolina with his wife Suzette, an antique and vintage expert, and their teenage daughters. Visit bobbatchelor.com.

Preface

Every day, we make countless choices that shape our lives. From the moment we wake up until we go to bed, we constantly make decisions that affect our health, relationships, career, and overall well-being. Some of the common choices we make in everyday life include:

1. We must choose what to eat for breakfast, lunch, and dinner. We also must choose whether to eat healthily or indulge in junk food.

2. We must choose what to wear depending on the weather, occasion, and our personal style.

3. We must choose how to spend our free time, whether to watch TV, read a book, or engage in a hobby.

4. We must choose whom to spend time with, whether it's family, friends, or acquaintances.

5. We must choose how to communicate with others, whether it's through face-to-face conversations, phone calls, or text messages.

6. We must choose where to live, whether it's in a big city or a small town, or whether to rent or buy a home.

7. We must choose how to spend our money, whether it's on necessities, entertainment, or saving for the future.

8. We must choose what career to pursue, which can shape our future and our overall happiness and fulfillment.

9. We must choose what goals to set for ourselves, whether personal, career, or relationship goals.

10. We must choose how to handle challenges and obstacles that come our way, whether it's through persistence, problem-solving, or seeking help and support from others.

This book is about the never-ending need we have to make choices. If you think about it, we must choose what time to wake up every morning, what to wear (unless we need to wear a uniform), what to have for breakfast (if we eat breakfast), lunch and dinner (and if we eat in restaurants, what to order), and our need to make all kinds of other choices all day long.

Some of our choices are mundane, like what to have for breakfast (if we eat breakfast): to have coffee or tea (and if so, plain or with milk), cereal, toast or a bagel (and if so, what kind: plain, with poppy seeds, with everything) or a sweet roll, eggs (if so, fried, soft boiled, scrambled), and so on. Most of the choices we make are not important, and we often develop habits to relieve us of having to think about our choices.

For example, I have the same thing for breakfast every day: a bowl of oatmeal with chia seeds and flax seeds, hot milk, a cup of espresso coffee with hot milk, and half a bagel with butter. Occasionally I have a soft-boiled egg, as well.

But other choices we must make are life changing, such as how to live (single, living with a partner, or getting married), what kind of education to get, what kind of job or profession to choose, where to live and what kind of house to buy (if you can afford a house), whom to vote for, and so on.

This book will help you understand, appreciate, and recognize the importance and the power of the choices we make in our everyday lives, in society and in culture.

Acknowledgments

I would like to thank all the writers, scholars, theorists, and others whose ideas and writings have informed this book. I like to quote from authors whose work I use so my readers can not only learn about their ideas but see how they express themselves. So, I don't paraphrase very often but use excerpts from their writings—but none longer than 300 words, so the quotations are all fair use.

I also owe a debt of gratitude to my editor, Blanca Caro Duran, and the production team at Vernon publishers for their help in producing this book.

List of Illustrations

Figure 1.1: Mary Douglas 3

Figure 2.1: Karl Marx 7

Figure 2.2: Henri Lefebvre 8

Figure 2.3: Everyday Life in the Modern World 9

Figure 2.4: Raymond Williams 9

Figure 3.1: Drawing in Journal 106 of BonsenKitchen 8001 Espresso Machine 11

Figure 3.2: BonsenKitchen $75 Espresso Machine 12

Figure 3.3: My various coffee makers 12

Figure 3.4: Breville Barista $850 14

Figure 3.5: DF464 $375 15

Figure 3.6: Rocket Fausto $1250 15

Figure 3.7: Krups flat burr coffee grinder. $50 16

Figure 3.8: The AFIM Conical Burr Grinder 16

Figure 3.9: Triestino Coffee 17

Figure 4.1: Pierre Bourdieu 21

Figure 4.2: Oatmeal and Hot Milk 23

Figure 4.3: Toasted Half Bagel and Latte 23

Figure 4.4: Bacon and Two Eggs on the *Royal Princess* 24

Figure 4.5: Emile Durkheim 28

Figure 5.1: Ferdinand de Saussure 36

Figure 5.2: Signifier/Signified. Berger, after Saussure 36

Figure 5.3: Charles Sanders Peirce 37

Figure 5.4: Aleph 38

Figure 5.5: Fidji perfume advertisement 41

Figure 6.1: Sigmund Freud 45

Figure 6.2: Representation of Consciousness, Subconsciousness and Unconsciousness 46

Figure 6.3: The Id, Ego and Superego. 47

Figure 6.4: Detail from United Airlines Advertisement 49

Figure 6.5: Joan Riviere   52

Figure 9.1: Our Living Room   71

Figure 9.2: Dining Room   72

Figure 10.1: Ocean Travel and Cruising   79

Figure 11.1: Judith Butler   86

Figure 12.1: Cover of Journal Number 106   91

Figure 12.2: Brainstorming on a Possible Book on Choices   92

Figure 12.3: Brainstorming Page on Choices   93

Figure 12.4: Mikhail Bakhtin   95

Figure 12.5: Labyrinth   96

List of Tables

Table 1.1:   The Four Lifestyles   5

Table 4.1:   Taste and Choice   21

Table 5.1:   Peirce's icon/index/symbol   38

Table 5.2:   Metaphor and Metonymy   40

Table 6.1:   Id, Ego and Superego   49

Table 6.2:   Id, Ego and Superego and Culture   50

Table 8.1:   Education and Work   63

Table 11.1: Male-Female Binary Oppositions   88

Takeways

In this book, you will learn about the ideas of some of the most important scholars, writers and theorists who have written about the subject of choices, and you will also read excerpts from their books and articles so you can see how they expressed themselves.

1.

Here, we learn about the ideas of Schopenhauer and Jonathan Edwards about human freedom and its relationship to choice. Schopenhauer wrote that "A man can do what he wants but not want what he wants," and Edwards, a Puritan minister, suggested that man can act as he pleases but not please as he pleases. He argued, in essence, that "All choices…are necessarily determined."

2.

In the Preface, I discuss the difference between mundane, everyday choices (such as what to have for breakfast) and very important choices, such as how to live (single, living with a partner, or getting married) or deciding on an occupation.

3.

In the epigraph to chapter 1, I discuss grid-group theory, which was developed by a British social anthropologist, Mary Douglas, and its relation to fatalism. Her thinking suggests that one choice we make, which involves what kind of lifestyle we choose (to the extent we can choose a lifestyle), shapes all of our other choices.

4.

Grid-group theory argues that there are four lifestyles that are based on the power of group boundaries and the number of rules and prescriptions one must obey. These two choices generate four lifestyles: hierarchical elitists, competitive individualists, egalitarians, and fatalists, all of which are antagonistic to the other lifestyles. It is these unrecognized imperatives in our lifestyles that shape much of our behavior and the choices we make.

5.

The epigraph to the next chapter, on Marxism and choice, explains how capitalist ideology shapes our thinking and how it is reflected in our popular culture and culture in general. This ideology, promulgated by the ruling classes, shapes our work, play, work patterns, relations between men and women, and customs of everyday life.

6.

I offer some selections from Marx's writings about how the ruling classes shape our thinking. He argues that the ideas of the ruling classes, which are promulgated in their interest, become accepted by the working classes or proletariat.

7.

A French Marxist, Henri Lefebvre, suggests that in capitalist societies, where the few (the ruling classes) rule the many (the masses, the proletariat), there is generally an element of compulsion that can lead to a state of terror. The cover of his book, *Everyday Life in the Modern World*, shows a kitchen table with a bowl of milk and some bowls, representing the world of everyday life for the ordinary person, and in the window, an atom bomb going off, representing the world of the powerful.

8.

Raymond Williams, an English Marxist, discusses the concept of hegemony, which explains why the working classes don't recognize the exploitation they experience. Hegemony is a broader concept than ideology and involves our entire system of practices and living and can be described as "that which goes without saying," which helps maintain the dominance of the ruling classes.

9.

Chapter 3 is a case study of Home Espresso Machine Aficionados who spend a great deal of time discussing their espresso machines and the many intricacies involved in pulling a great espresso shot. Many of the members of this internet club spend thousands of dollars on their coffee bean grinders and espresso machines in search of what they call the "God" shot. I became interested in this club and the whole espresso machine lovers phenomenon when I purchased an inexpensive machine and saw a posting from a member of the club (which I joined) on Facebook. The club members divide the world into minimalists, like me, who have inexpensive espresso machines, and maximalists, who spend many hundreds and, in some cases, thousands of dollars on their passion.

10.

The enormous number of espresso brands brings up the question of choice. There are many kinds and brands of espresso machines and grinders and one of the problems facing someone wishing to purchase an espresso machine is what kind of machine to get and what brand is best. When there are so many kinds and brands of espresso machines, we confront the tyranny of choice. You can become paralyzed by having so many choices. This leads people planning to purchase a machine to look on the Internet at sites about "best espresso machines" and espresso gurus who can be found on YouTube.

11.

Social Choice Theories deal with collective decision making and how groups of individuals can choose the best political candidates, welfare systems, and so on. It asks how we turn a collection of individual choices into collective outputs.

12.

We can distinguish between taste and choice. Taste is what we like, and choice is what we buy or get, based on our income, the degree to which our rational way of decision-making shapes our thinking and behavior and other factors such as the role of fads and influencers.

13.

The French sociologist Pierre Bourdieu writes in *Sociology in Question,* "Sociology reveals that the idea of personal opinion (like the idea of personal taste) is an illusion." Taste is shaped by social forces, education and other factors. We can say the same thing about choices, except that taste is what we like, or desire, and choice is what we buy.

14.

I offer, as a case study, my choices for breakfast. People often develop habits or routines to make life easier for them, which is what I've done for my breakfasts. I have the same breakfast just about every day and have followed my routine for many years.

15.

Another case study involving choices deals with the choice of a home to purchase. It is usually our largest purchase and investment. Because there are so many factors involved, purchasing a home is often an ordeal, and it is not unusual for people shopping for a home to visit 30 or 40 different homes that are on the market.

16.

A marketing firm, Claritas, has developed an elaborate typology based on the zip codes where people live, arguing that "birds of a feather flock together." What we find is that people in the same socio-economic status tend to live near each other and some zip codes have very expensive homes in them while others have middle-class or lower-class homes. Claritas lists some sixty distinct kinds of people, with jazzy names such as "01: Upper Crust Wealthy Mature w/o Kids" based on their preferences, lifestyles, and income.

17.

The Claritas typology suggests a typology of life choices, which involved occupations, marriage or non-marriage, education, house location, brands of automobiles, religions, political affiliations, and everyday life choices such as clothes, food preferences, pop culture, sports and so on.

18.

Semiotics, the science of signs, is now an important tool of marketing and, therefore, plays a role in the choices we make in many areas. Signs, according to Ferdinand des Saussure, one of the founding fathers of the science, are composed of a sound or object or image (a *signifier*) and the meaning of that signifier (a *signified*). To understand how to interpret signs, we must know the codes that give the signs meaning.

19.

Semiotics argues that whatever we do sends messages to others in a variety of codes. As Maya Pines, a journalist, explains, "we are always "on the receiving end of innumerable messages encoded in music, gestures, foods, rituals, books, movies, or advertisements." But we don't realize that we have received these messages and can't explain the rules by which they operate. That is where semiotics comes in.

20.

Charles Sanders Peirce, an American philosopher who was a professor at Harvard and the other founding father of semiotics, suggested that there were three kinds of signs: icons (based on resemblance), indexes (based on causal connections) and symbols (whose meaning we must learn).

21.

From a semiotic perspective, we can look at the brands we choose to generate a "self" (which leads to our sense of our "selves"} as tied to the quality, cost, etc., of the brands of things we purchase and to distinguish ourselves from others based on our brands. A brand is a sign or symbol that identifies the goods a seller has and differentiates the brand from competitors.

22.

Advertisers and marketers use linguistic devices such as metaphor and metonymy, symbols, visual persuasion devices and whatever they can to attract the attention of people and sell them whatever products or services that the advertisers offer.

23.

An analysis of a Fidji perfume with a snake around the model's neck, holding a bottle of Fidji, suggests that advertisements often have symbols and hidden meanings that affect those exposed to them. In this ad, there are many sexual symbols, and it is even possible that the word sex is shown in the snake's curve, the horizontals found at the top and bottom of the perfume bottle, and the way the woman in the ad is holding the bottle.

24.

A quotation from an article on semiotics and brands by Laura Oswald discusses the role of semiotics in creating brands and the power of symbolic representations to shape consumer preferences.

25.

A book by an English writer, Chris Hackley, *Marketing in Context*, deals with the role of marketing by giant corporations in shaping consumer choices. He writes, "We may face the massive promotional resources of global corporations telling us what our happy lifestyle should look like, but in the end, we are free to choose." Some scholars who write about consumer cultures question how much freedom to choose we actually have.

26.

The chapter on "Choice and the Psyche" offers a primer on relevant psychoanalytic concepts as they relate to the matter of choice. It discusses some of Freud's ideas about the three levels of consciousness (the conscious, preconscious, and unconscious) and three forces working in the psyche (the Id, Ego, and Superego) which play an important role in our behavior and the choices we make.

27.

The psyche's three levels can be represented by an iceberg, with consciousness being the small tip of the iceberg showing above the water, the subconscious (or preconscious) being a few feet of the iceberg below the water, and the unconscious being something like 90% of the iceberg that we cannot see. What is important is to recognize that there are hidden imperatives in the unconscious that shape our behavior and our thinking.

28.

A marketing professor at Harvard, Gerald Zaltman, argues in his book on how customers think, that "At least 95 percent of all cognition occurs below awareness in the shadows of the mind, while at most, only 5 percent occurs in high-level consciousness."

29.

We can use Freud's theory about the battle in our psyches to suggest that our choices are shaped, in large measure, by the Id, which is a cauldron of surging emotions. A United Airlines advertisement (reprinted in the book) shows the battle between the Id and the Superego. The Id is dominated by cravings and the Superego by restraint. The Ego, which represents rationality, mediates between these two forces.

30.

We can use Freud's Id/Ego/Superego typology to deal with many aspects of life, such as book genres, cities, heroes, TV shows, and so on.

31.

Freud wrote about the various defense mechanisms the ego uses to deal with pressures from the Id and the Superego, such as ambivalence, rationalization, and fixation. There is also the element of "Buyer's Regret" or "Buyer's Remorse," which many people feel about the choices they have made when purchasing products and services. These forces are internal and counter the elation we often feel after we have made a choice.

32.

Joan Riviere, an English psychoanalyst, explains in "Hate, Greed and Aggression" that greed occurs in everyone and that ultimately, our desire for good things is based upon demonstrating in the depths of our minds that we are good and worthy of love.

33.

The song "Falling in Love Again," made famous by Marlene Dietrich, introduces us to the matter of choosing a partner (wife, husband, someone to live with), which is one of the most consequential actions or choices we can take. The word "falling" suggests a lack of control and an inability to determine how the fall will end and what its consequences might be. There is an element of terror involved in any kind of falling since we've lost our ability to choose the fall's resolution.

34.

An English psychoanalyst, Melanie Klein, writes in "Love, Greed and Aggression," about the way love shapes our relationship with others and how having a sexual partner, generally in marriage, is felt by people to be a a signifier and reassurance of their goodness.

35.

Marriage is a cultural universal and approximately 4 to 5 million people get married in the United States every year, but around 42 to 53 percentage of marriages end in divorce. So, there is a considerable element of risk involved in getting married, and divorce can be seen as a form of "buyer's remorse." Since around half of marriages end in divorce, many couples don't get married but live together and many have children. These statistics come from data on the Internet.

36.

The average marriage lasts around eight years before couples get divorced and the legal fees for getting a divorce cost around $15,000. People contemplate getting divorced for around a year before they file for divorce.

37.

Elizabeth Blake is the author of an article, "Single? You're Not Alone," about the fact that not everyone searches for romantic relationships and many people like living alone. She adds, "more Americans are living unmarried and without a romantic partner," because they feel that living alone is more conducive to personal self-development and autonomy. Her article appeared on a website, *The Conversation,* on February 1, 2023.

38.

This discussion of work points out the difference between those with college educations and those with high school educations. It quotes the story of creation in which Adam and Eve were in paradise but were expelled for eating from the tree of knowledge and forcing Adam to work. As God put it, "In the seat of thy face shalt thou eat bread."

39.

Karl Marx had important things to say about work and the alienation of workers from themselves and their work. He argued work was external to workers and is not fulfilling, as well as often being physically exhausting and mentally debasing. He writes about workers, "The life which he has given to the object sets itself against him as an alien and hostile force." This leads to workers experiencing themselves as objects.

40.

An article, "When Workers Feel Like Objects: A Field Study on Self-Objectification and Affective Commitment" (by Roberta Rosa Valtorta and Maria Grazia Monaci in the *Europe Journal of Psychology*), offers a more modern assessment of the alienation of workers and the way they are treated as objects.

41.

The debate about whether Marx should be understood as a humanist, focusing on alienation, or as a revolutionary is discussed. It is a subject that Marxists, from both perspectives, continue to dispute.

42.

An article in the *Washington Post* on changes to the work week suggests important changes are coming to the workweek and many people support the four-day work week. Because of the COVID-19 outbreak, many workers now work from home and some only come into their offices one or two days a week.

43.

Finding a home (or apartment) to purchase is one of the largest investments most people make, and it is not unusual for people looking for a house to buy to visit dozens of homes looking for one that they like and can afford. In many cases, it is a traumatic experience. Often, people who purchase a home make major transformations in their new homes before they move into them.

44.

Dean MacCannell's definition of the tourist as an exemplar of contemporary society suggests that tourism is more important than most people think it is. His book, *The Tourist,* is considered a classic study of tourism and its role in society and culture.

45.

An important typology of kinds of tourists by an Israeli sociologist, Erik Cohen, deals with many kinds of tourists. The organized mass tourists in Cohen's typology take group tours and have relatively little opportunity to do things on their own or interact with people, not on the tour.

46.

One of the most influential typologies about tourism developed by Stanley Plog which characterizes them by their psychological state and ability to deal with anxiety and stress.

47.

In recent years, American attitudes about members of the LGBTQIA+ community have found increased acceptance, though many religiously and politically conservative Americans do not, and many members and leaders of the Republican Party attack them with punitive legislation. There is an increasing number of hate crimes against them, which suggests that some people cannot accept the community.

48.

According to a Gallup poll, around 7% of adults in America identify as LGBT, 86% are heterosexual or "straight," and 7% refuse to disclose their gender identity. Approximately half of the LGBT are bisexual. What these figures reveal is that many millions of adult Americans, approximately 20 million, are LGBT. Some 13 million Americans, 13 and above, identity as transgender.

49.

The Russian communications theorist, Mikhail Bakhtin, explained that language is dialogic. He suggested words used in the past affect words that will be used in the future in conversations and texts from the past often affect new texts of all kinds, a concept known as intertextuality.

50.

Jorge Luis Borges wrote a famous story, "The Garden of Forking Paths," which offers us a metaphor that captures the essence of having to make a choice: which path, when we come to forking paths, do we choose? He mentions the term "labyrinth" in his story and its image shows us, visually, the dilemmas we face as we wander through the "labyrinths" of everyday life.

PART ONE:
THEORIES

Grid and Group cultural theory (Cultural Theory) was developed over the past thirty years through the work of British anthropologists Mary Douglas and Michael Thompson. This theory addresses the level of an individual in an organization. It attempts to explain the changes both within and between dimensions and deals with dynamism (Thompson et al., 1990). Cultural Theory has been used to study the different views of environmental and technological risks in society....The Cultural Theory framework has two dimensions, namely, the Grid and the Group. The Grid dimension refers to the degree to which a social context is regulated and restrictive in regard to the individuals' behaviour, while the Group dimension refers to an individual as a member of bonded social units, *specifically on 'how absorbing the group's activities are on the individual'*....The two dimensions give four different cultural views with distinct ways of life or world views.

Fatalism is a view held by individuals who have a weak bond with other people (Thompson et al., 1990). They are strong in Grid, which may have many and varied interpersonal differences. They are left to their own fates, which may be positive or negative for them. Values related to fatalism are apathy and isolation. Hierarchism is a view held by people with control and a strong Grid and Group, which reflect the control and power values. They are strongly connected yet are very different. This leads to the development of institutions, hierarchies, and laws that both regulate individual actions and provide for weaker social members....In the Individualism view, people are relatively similar, yet have little obligation to one another. People enjoy their differences more than their similarities and seek to avoid central authority.

Library.net. (n.d.). "Grid and group cultural theory and organisational culture."

Chapter 1

The Social-Anthropology of Choice

This chapter deals with the choices that shape other choices and is based on the work of social anthropologist Mary Douglas and other scholars who used her theories in their work.

The Choices That Shape All Other Choices:
Grid-Group Theory

Before we discuss grid-group theory, let me say something about the ideas of Jonathan Edwards on choice. One of America's greatest thinkers, the Puritan minister Jonathan Edwards, wrestled with the problem of free will (choice) and determinism (an all-powerful God). He solved the problem by suggesting that people live in two realms: one is action, and the other is choice. In the realm of action, we can do whatever we want, at least in theory. In the realm of choice, things are different. While we can act as we please, we cannot please as we please, for it is an all-powerful God who determines what pleases us. So, the idea that we can choose freely is a delusion, since it is God who determines what pleases us.

Figure 1.1: Mary Douglas

There is a theory developed by social anthropologist Mary Douglas, who argues that our choices are not as free as we think they are. Her work has been very influential in several scholarly areas.

Grid-group Theory argues that there are four "lifestyles," and everyone in modern societies is a member of one of these lifestyles, whether they recognize they are or not.

In their 1990 book *Cultural Theory*, Michael Thompson, Richard Ellis, and Aaron Wildavsky discuss the ways in which political cultures are formed. Their ideas are based on what is known as *grid-group theory*, which was developed by Douglas. Thompson et al. discuss the main points that Douglas makes in her presentation of this theory (1990, 5):

> She argues that the variability of an individual's involvement in social life can be adequately captured by two dimensions of sociality: group and grid. *Group* refers to the extent to which an individual is incorporated into bounded units. The greater the incorporation, the more individual choice is subject to group determination. *Grid* denotes the degree to which an individual's life is circumscribed by externally imposed prescriptions. The more binding and extensive the scope of the prescriptions, the less of life that is open to individual negotiation.

What Douglas calls the group dimension involves the degree to which membership in a group shapes and sustains an individual's life. The influence of a group on a person can be weak or strong. The grid dimension deals with whether individuals must obey many rules and prescriptions or just a few of them. In their book, Thompson et al. describe how this grid-group typology leads to four political cultures or ways of life (1990, 6-7):

> Strong group boundaries coupled with minimal prescriptions produce social relations that are egalitarian....When an individual's social environment is characterized by strong group boundaries and binding prescriptions, the resulting social relations are hierarchical. . . . Individuals who are bound by neither group incorporation nor prescribed roles inhabit an individualistic social context. In such an environment, all boundaries are provisional and subject to negotiation....People who find themselves subject to binding prescriptions and are excluded from group membership exemplify the fatalistic way of life. Fatalists are controlled from without.

These four different ways of life are antagonistic to each other, but they all need one another. *Hierarchical elitists* believe in stratification and in the responsibility of those at the top to look after those below them. *Individualists* are interested primarily in themselves and want the freedom to compete fairly protected by the government. *Egalitarians* stress that people are equal in terms of their needs and that differences among people are social and not natural and should be played down. *Fatalists* believe in luck and opt out of the political system. All four groups are locked into complementary relationships, and all are necessary for the political order. If we take the two dimensions—group membership (weak or strong) and grid aspects (few or many rules and prescriptions)—we can see how they generate the four ways of life or political cultures:

Table 1.1: The Four Lifestyles

Way of Life	Group Boundaries	Prohibitions
Hierarchal Elitist	Strong	Numerous and Varied
Egalitarian	Strong	Few
Competitive Individualist	Weak	Few
Fatalist	Weak	Numerous and Varied

Table by the author

According to Thompson et al., social scientists are always looking for latent or hidden aspects of social phenomena. The authors use this insight to offer a comment on the Marxist view of societies (1990, 149):

> Things are never as they seem in class societies, Marx tells us, because exploitation must be disguised for the social order to be sustained. Since rulers do not like to think of themselves as exploiters, benefiting unjustly from the labor of others, and the exploited must be kept ignorant of their subjection lest they revolt, the truth must be kept from both rulers and ruled alike.

They argue that Marx ties mystification to the capitalist economic system, and they suggest that mystification pervades every aspect of life, and it is the task of the social scientist to explore and explain this mystification.

We can see that egalitarians are like Marxists in stressing that everyone should be treated the same way and has the same needs. But what Marx didn't recognize, Thompson et al. assert, is that egalitarianism can function as a useful critique of social relationships and arrangements only when it is out of power. If Marx had analyzed egalitarian political cultures as well as hierarchist and fatalist ones (read here as "bourgeois" and "proletarian"), these authors suggest he would have developed different theories about sociopolitical institutions and the need for revolution.

Applied to any aspect of culture, Marxist method seeks to explicate the manifest and latent or coded reflections of modes of material production, ideological values, class relations and structures of social power—racial or sexual as well as politico-economic—or the state of consciousness of people in a precise historical or socio-economic situation....The Marxist method, recently in varying degrees of combination with structuralism and semiology, has provided an incisive analytic tool for studying the political signification in every facet of contemporary culture, including popular entertainment in TV and films, music, mass circulation books, newspaper and magazine features, comics, fashion, tourism, sports and games, as well as such acculturating institutions as education, religion, the family and child-rearing, social and sexual relations between men and women—all the patterns of work, play, and other customs of everyday life....The most frequent theme in Marxist cultural criticism is the way the prevalent mode of production and the ideology of the ruling class in any society dominate every phase of culture, and at present, the way capitalist production and ideology dominate American culture, along with that of the rest of the world that American business and culture have colonized. This domination is perpetuated both through overt propaganda in political rhetoric, news reporting, advertising, and public relations, and through the often unconscious absorption of capitalistic values by creators and consumers in all the above aspects of the culture of everyday life.

Donald Lazere. 1977. "Mass culture, political consciousness, and English studies." *College English.* (755-756)

Chapter 2

Marxism and Choices

Figure 2.1: Karl Marx

Marxists have important things to say about choices, but they use different terms when dealing with them. Marx discusses what he describes as false consciousness, which involves how the ruling classes shape the thinking of the working classes or proletariat. It is important for the ruling classes to affect people's consciousness by giving them certain ideas; in this way, the ruling classes, who benefit most from the social arrangements in capitalist countries, maintain the status quo. Marx (1964) explains (in Bottomore and Sobel's *Selected Writings in sociology and social philosophy*) how the ruling class operates (1964, 78):

> The ideas of the ruling class are, in every age, the ruling ideas: i.e., the class which is the dominant *material* force in society is at the same time its dominant *intellectual* force. The class which has the means of material production at its disposal, has control at the same time over the means of mental production, so that in consequence the ideas of those who lack the means of mental production are, in general, subject to it. The dominant ideas are nothing more than the ideal expression of the dominant material relationships, the dominant material relationships grasped as ideas, and thus of the relationships which make one class the ruling one; they are consequently the ideas of its dominance. The individuals composing the ruling class possess among other things consciousness, and, therefore, think. Insofar, therefore, as they rule as a class and determine the whole extent of an epoch, it is self-evident that they do this in their whole range and thus, among other things, rule also as thinkers, as producers of ideas, and regulate the production and distribution of the ideas of their age. Consequently, their ideas are the ruling ideas of their age.

What this means is that the ideas of an age are those promulgated and popularized by the ruling class in its own interest. The ideas people have are, Marxists argue, the ideas that the ruling class wants them to have, and this ultimately affects the proletariat's choices in many aspects of their lives.

Marx explained that capitalism generates alienation and a sense of estrangement from others and, ultimately, from themselves. The ruling classes have found a way to deal with this alienation by channeling the alienation of members of the proletariat into mass consumption by creating consumer cultures, in which people dealt with their alienation by consuming products and services and by creating a society of spectacle.

Members of the proletariat focus their attention on making choices among the things they can buy, hoping that these choices will lead to a better life and shield them from the alienation and estrangement they feel.

They do this because they have accepted the ideologies spread by the members of the ruling classes and the writers and artists who work for them in promulgating their ideological beliefs hidden in popular culture, the media, and other aspects of everyday life.

Figure 2.2: Henri Lefebvre

HEVRI LEFEBVRE

A French Marxist, Henri Lefebvre, argues that in capitalist countries, the proletariat lives in a state of terror. He says that in any country in which there are radical class differences, in which a small group of people are at the top and the masses at the bottom, control must be maintained through compulsion and persuasion. In these highly stratified situations, the ruling class finds itself required to become overly repressive and develops ways of making members of the proletariat the instruments of their own repression and the repression of others.

This leads to a "terrorist" society in which (1984:147):

> Compulsion and the illusion of freedom converge; unacknowledged compulsions besiege the lives of communities (and of their individual members) and organize them according to a general strategy...in a terrorist society terror is diffuse, violence is always latent, pressure is exerted from all sides on its members, who can only avoid and shift its weight it by a super-human effort.

The cover of his book, *Everyday Life in the Modern World*, is very interesting.

Figure 2.3: Everyday Life in the Modern World

It shows two worlds: the world of everyday life, as represented by a bottle of milk and bowls on the kitchen table, and the world of the powerful, as represented by the atomic bomb shown exploding in the window.

Figure 2.4: Raymond Williams

The decisions of the masses are confined to choices they make about food to purchase and other personal matters, while the big decisions are made by the ruling elites, whose power is represented by the atomic bomb they have just set off.

Marxist thinkers like Raymond Williams, an English scholar, use Gramsci's concept of hegemony to explain why people cannot recognize their true status. Williams writes, in *Marxism and Literature* (1977, 109-119):

> It is distinct in its refusal to equate consciousness with the articulate formal system which can be and ordinarily is abstracted as "ideology." It, of course, does not exclude the articulate and formal meanings, values, and beliefs which a dominant class develops and propagates. But it does not equate these with consciousness, or rather, it does not reduce consciousness to them. Instead, it sees the relations of dominance and subordination, in their forms, as practical consciousness, as in effect, a saturation of the whole process of living—not only of political and economic activity, nor only of manifest social activity, but of the whole substance of lived identities and relationships, to such a depth that the pressures and limits of what can ultimately be seen as a specific economic, political and cultural system seem to most of us the pressures and limits of simple experience and common sense. Hegemony is then not only the articulate upper level of "ideology," nor are its forms of control only those ordinarily seen as "manipulation" or "indoctrination." It is a whole body of practices and expectations, over the whole of living: our senses, our assignments of energy, our shaping perceptions of ourselves and our world. It is a lived system of meanings and values—constitutive and constituting—which, as they are experienced as practices, appear as reciprocally confirming. It thus constitutes a sense of reality for most people in the society, a sense of the absolute because experienced reality beyond which it is very difficult for most members of the society to move in most areas of their lives.

We can describe hegemony as "that which goes without saying," or the givens or commonsense realities of the world, which, it turns out, serve an ultimate purpose—that of maintaining the dominance of the ruling class. The mass media carry works that can be seen not merely as carriers of ideology that manipulate and indoctrinate people with certain views. The media are unwitting instruments of hegemonic domination and have a much broader and deeper influence—they shape people's very ideas about themselves and the world; they shape people's worldviews.

And it is our worldviews that shape our desires and the choices we make to satisfy these desires. We should not underestimate the passion with which people pursue their interest in their purchases, as the following discussion, a case study of home espresso machine lovers, shows.

Chapter 3

Espresso Machine Aficionados:

A Case Study

Let me begin with my introduction to the world of espresso machine addicts and obsessives.

Moving Up to an Espresso Coffee Maker

On Tuesday, September 20th, 2023, I made a drawing in my journal of a BonsenKitchen 8001 espresso machine. I chose it after exploring the various espresso machines on sale at Amazon.com, which range from around fifty dollars to many thousands of dollars. I paid around $75 for it by ordering it directly from the Bonsenkitchen website.

Figure 3.1: Drawing in Journal 106 of BonsenKitchen 8001 Espresso Machine

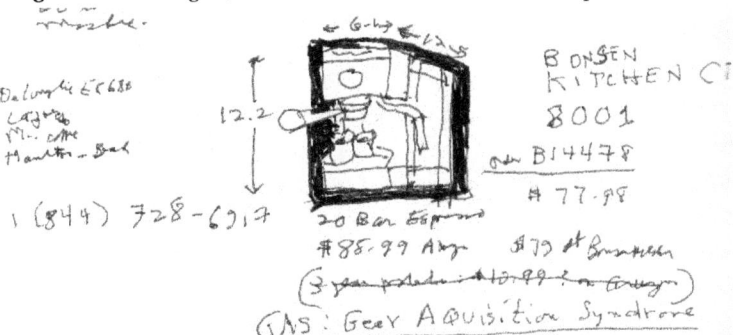

In 1963, I spent a year in Italy as a Fulbright scholar teaching at the University of Milan. I got used to excellent coffee while there. While in Italy, I bought a three-cup stovetop Bialetti espresso maker that I used there and in America when I returned in 1964.

Many people use this kind of espresso maker, but it is not really a device that produces espresso, which we will understand to be coffee with a crema. What the Bialetti does is make very strong coffee, which is better than the coffee one gets with percolators.

Figure 3.2: BonsenKitchen $75 Espresso Machine

After many years using the Bialetti, I graduated to a Bella steam Espresso maker. It isn't a real espresso machine in that the coffee it makes doesn't have a crema, but it makes very strong coffee. I believe I paid something like $35 for it. And then, in September 2022, I decided to get a "real" espresso machine.

Figure 3.3: My various coffee makers

Why I did so is a bit of an enigma. Why people make certain choices is a fascinating topic and one that is the subject of an enormous amount of effort by marketing companies, advertising agencies, food companies, companies that are part of American consumer culture, governmental agencies, and many other people in all kinds of different organizations.

Maybe I found myself in a buying mood? Our kitchen stove and refrigerator both had to be replaced and perhaps choosing a new stove and refrigerator put me into a buying mindset?

When I started looking for espresso machines on Amazon.com, I was surprised at how many machines it sold and how expensive some home espresso machines were. I was still using an ordinary grinder to grind the coffee beans I purchased at Costco and had a very primitive set up.

The Home Espresso Machine Aficionados

One day, while cruising the Internet, I came across an organization of Home Espresso Machine Aficionados, which was a virtual community of espresso lovers. Some might say fanatics. My daughter, who is a psychoanalyst, suggested "obsessives." What I discovered was that if someone in the association asked a question, forty or fifty members of the association might offer an answer. Many of the questions involved what model or espresso machine or burr grinder to purchase and opinions varied wildly on what the best device to get was, based on price ranges and similar considerations. My daughter bought me a flat burr grinder for $50 for my 90th birthday, so now I have a "set up" that cost $125.

The ideal goal for these espresso lovers was what they called a "God shot" of espresso. And this espresso was not to be consumed with milk. If you did that, you were relegated to a different status from the "God shot" seekers.

I discovered, later, that there is another association of beginning Espresso lovers, which also had members who were quite passionate about Espresso. I also joined it. And then I found that there are also clubs or virtual communities of people who own certain brands of home Espresso makers and companies that sell used Espresso machines and grinders. There are many videos about Espresso machines on YouTube, as well.

Since I am curious about the different espresso machines, I now get many advertisements on Facebook selling these devices: sometimes from the brand itself and sometimes from stores specializing in Espresso machines or companies like Amazon or Walmart. There are also many lists on the Internet that deal with different espresso machines, brands of espresso machines, and grinders for these devices.

In short, there are a bewildering number of choices one must make about espresso machines depending on one's mindset and budget. My theory is to keep it simple, so I am spared the anxiety and stress that people who are really serious about the espresso experience feel. My machine produces an espresso that is good enough for me. I add a bit of milk and zap the coffee and milk in my microwave to produce a decent latte. At the other extreme, we have those in search of "God shots" and who experience endless problems and anxieties in their search. When you get involved with God, it seems there are always mystifications and complications.

Recently, I came across a posting on Facebook from someone asking members of the Aficionados a question about which espresso machine to buy and there were 81 replies, with many brands and models suggested by members. Many of the posts on the Aficionados site involve experiences with different models and brands of espresso machines and grinders.

What is Choice?

Choice involves the ability to choose between or among alternatives. We often think of choice in terms of binary oppositions: good versus evil, safe versus dangerous, and so on. With espresso machines and related devices, however, we have an enormous number of alternatives to consider.

Coffee Affection lists fifteen different types of espresso machines:

> **What are the types of espresso machines?** There are 15 varieties, including differences in water flow (reservoir, direct connect, and volumetric espresso machines) and differences in boilers (single boiler, double boiler, and heat exchanging espresso machines). There are also differences in mechanism (lever, steam-driven, and pump-driven espresso machines), and levels of automatic operation (semi-automatic, automatic, super-automatic, ultra-automatic espresso machines). Finally, you have pod espresso machines and stovetop espresso machines.

In addition, there are countless brands, some with many models available with different mechanisms in them, so there are an enormous number of things to consider if you want a machine other than a basic model.

Various members have written that you cannot get a real espresso machine for less than $600 and you must spend as much on your grinder as you spend on your espresso machine.

Figure 3.4: Breville Barista $850

Consider the difference between my espresso machine and the one with all the dials and other devices, which cost many hundreds of dollars more.

Once you move above a "keep it simple, stupid" basic espresso machine, you face an almost infinite number of choices, which means decisions you must make about which advanced home espresso machine to purchase and what you must do when making an espresso shot with that machine.

Incidentally, the Breville Barista espresso machine is not considered an expensive one and many members of the Aficionados have grinders that are more expensive than the Breville Barista.

Members of the club constantly write that one should decide upon a coffee grinder before deciding which espresso machine to get. The members write a great deal about their experiences with grinders and their desire to get a better grinder.

Many members of the club are animated by getting better espresso machines and better grinders and spend a lot of time discussing which machines to get and which grinders to get for their next step up the ladder of espresso devices.

There are also scales to buy and other things you need to use fancy espresso machines, all of which have become increasingly expensive.

Figure 3.5: DF464 $375   **Figure 3.6**: Rocket Fausto $1250

I started with a $15 grinder for all kinds of foods and then moved up to a $50 flat burr coffee grinder, which, as I mentioned earlier, was a birthday gift from my daughter. Members of the Aficionados all stress the importance of having a burr coffee grinder, and preferably a round burr grinder, so they would look down on my choice of a Krups flat burr grinder.

When I decided to buy a burr coffee grinder, I looked on Amazon to see what was available and noticed that thousands of people had purchased Krups grinders, so I chose it, assuming that there might be a good reason why so many people like it. Has it made a great deal of difference in the quality of my espressos? Hard to say, but with espresso, minor improvements are important.

Figure 3.7: Krups flat burr coffee grinder. $50

My setup: espresso machine and coffee grinder cost $125 and I can get decent espressos with it. Since I add milk to my espressos, the purists in the Aficionados have relegated me to the hell reserved for people not "serious" about espressos, not searching for a "God shot."

Here is a recent post from a member of the Aficionados:

> I got into home espresso almost two years ago. I've been using the Breville Barista Express since I started, but I'm wanting to upgrade. My budget is roughly $1200 for a machine and a grinder. Thoughts and suggestions are welcome. I'm not opposed to getting used equipment if that's the best option.
>
> 39 comments.

The 39 comments all differed in terms of what was suggested. What is important to recognize is that many posts from Aficionado members get fifty or sixty comments from the members, which suggests that the Aficionado members are very alert and very serious about different aspects of the home espresso experience.

Figure 3.8: The AFIM Conical Burr Grinder

Many of the comments suggested different brands and models of espresso machines for the person making the post and everyone stressed the importance of getting a premium grinder before buying an espresso machine. For those who have fallen into the rabbit hole of upgrading their devices, the AFIM grinder at $1995 awaits.

We can see one can spend enormous amounts of money on espresso machines and grinders. With espresso, one can be a minimalist like me, and get a low-cost espresso machine and grinder, or a maximalist and spend an enormous amount of money in search of a "God" shot.

Coffee Espresso Machine Aficionados devote a considerable amount of attention to the kinds of coffee beans they purchase, and their filings mention many kinds of exotic coffee beans they use, all from the Arabica family of coffee beans.

There has been a revolution in the coffee industry and the dominance of Arabica coffee beans is now threatened by the rise of the Robusta beans, previously scorned by most coffee drinkers.

Home espresso makers talk about coffee beans the same way that wine lovers talk about wine and discuss matters such as "notes" of chocolate and being balanced.

Figure 3.9: Triestino Coffee

Here is what Triestino Espresso writes about itself:

Triestino Espresso is inspired by the coffee styles of Trieste, Italy – capital city of the Friuli Venezia Giulia region in Northeast Italy. The Port of Trieste is Italy's and one of Europe's great coffee ports, supplying more than 40% of Italy's coffee. Lighter bodied than our more traditional espresso blends with a smooth body and creamy mouthfeel, the rich nut-toned flavors of this blend are accented by lively fruit notes. The influence of the city's longstanding ties to Austria come through in this Triestino Blend.

Triestino Espresso | Roast level: MEDIUM-LIGHT | Cupping notes: Cashew, Raspberry Jam....

This advertisement for Triestino coffee is a good example of the kind of language used by coffee lovers in choosing what brand and kind of coffee to purchase.

A front-page article by Jon Emont in *The Wall Street Journal* on February 9, 2023, titled, "Bitter, Scorned Coffee Bean Seeks New Respect from Java Snobs," explains that many coffee lovers now are favoring Robusta beans:

> A younger generation of coffee geeks…thinks the time is ripe for a Robusta reputation reboot. They want to elevate the humble bean from the instant-coffee market to the premium coffee universe. Old-school coffee snobs are highly dubious.…The revisionist crowd argues that Robusta can be good if grown and processed with the same care as Arabica. They say premium Robusta is nutty and creamy—and lacks the rubbery taste that characterizes the cheaper stuff. Even better, Robusta is half the price of Arabica, although for premium beans the prices are closer.

Emont discusses the UK's Black Sheep Coffee company which has played an important role in the new popularity of the Robusta bean. He quotes one of the co-founders of the company on Arabica beans (2023, A10):

> The whole specialty coffee scene was so stuck in its ways that they would really look down on us.

Emont adds (2023, A10):

> He sees his nutty, chocolaty Robustas as a corrective for a speciality coffee culture that prizes acidic Arabica. "You would taste a coffee and it would taste like lemon juice," he said of Arabia. "Your average person would not enjoy it, and you'd have a super-geek barista who would tell you that, actually, no, that's the way real coffee is supposed to taste.

We can see that getting a good cup of coffee is a much more complicated matter than one might imagine. There are so many brands of espresso machines and coffee grinders and so many brands of coffee beans, which makes what used to be relatively simple, now become, for many coffee lovers, an ordeal. There was a recent article in *The New York Times* about other coffee varieties that are becoming popular because the drought has made growing Robustas increasingly difficult.

As for me, as a minimalist, I turn on my inexpensive espresso machine, have it rumble a bit, and then pours coffee into a glass. After an ounce or so has poured into the glass, I turn the espresso machine off, add another ounce or two of milk, zap it in my microwave, and enjoy it—even if it is far removed from the "God shot" that the Aficionados seek. Best is the enemy of good, or of good enough, for coffee and many other things.

Social Choice Theory

Social choice theory is the study of collective decision procedures and mechanisms. It is not a single theory, but a cluster of models and results concerning the aggregation of individual inputs (e.g., votes, preferences, judgments, welfare) into collective outputs (e.g., collective decisions, preferences, judgments, welfare). Central questions are: How can a group of individuals choose a winning outcome (e.g., policy, electoral candidate) from a given set of options? What are the properties of different voting systems? When is a voting system democratic? How can a collective (e.g., electorate, legislature, collegial court, expert panel, or committee) arrive at coherent collective preferences or judgments on some issues, on the basis of its members' individual preferences or judgments? How can we rank different social alternatives in an order of social welfare? Social choice theorists study these questions not just by looking at examples, but by developing general models and proving theorems.

Pioneered in the eighteenth century by Nicolas de Condorcet and Jean-Charles de Borda and in the nineteenth century by Charles Dodgson (also known as Lewis Carroll), social choice theory took off in the twentieth century with the works of Kenneth Arrow, Amartya Sen, and Duncan Black. Its influence extends across economics, political science, philosophy, mathematics, and, recently, computer science and biology. Apart from contributing to our understanding of collective decision procedures, social choice theory has applications in the areas of institutional design, welfare economics, and social epistemology.

Stanford Encyclopedia of Philosophy. (n.d.). "Social choice theory."

Chapter 4

The Sociology of Choice

There is a difference between taste and choice. Taste involves what we like, and choice involves how we operationalize taste and make decisions based not only on taste but other factors as well.

Table 4.1: Taste and Choice

TASTE	CHOICE
What you like	What you get
Desire	Income
Id	Ego

Table by the Author

Choice is the public face of taste, and there are times when our choices don't mesh with our tastes. Taste is what you like, and choice is what you end up with. Sometimes, your choices match your taste, but often, our choices aren't the same. You may really like Porsches but end up with Toyota Corollas or Honda Civics in your garage.

Think, for example, of our food choices. We might like fatty meat, but because of the problems we face with such foods, we may avoid this kind of food. Our doctors and dieticians may affect our food choices, but not our taste choices.

Figure 4.1: Pierre Bourdieu

Personal Opinion and Personal Taste

So choice, then, is not purely personal, and what we do is often constrained by other considerations. We can say the same for taste. As the French sociologist Pierre Bourdieu explains in his book, *Sociology in Question* (1993, 27):

Sociology reveals that the idea of personal opinion (like the idea of personal taste) is an illusion. From this, it is concluded that sociology is reductive, that it disenchants, that it demobilizes people by taking away all their illusions....If it is true that the idea of personal opinion itself is socially determined, that it is a product of history reproduced by education, that our opinions are determined, then it is better to know this; and if we have some chance of having personal opinions, it is perhaps on condition that we know our opinions are not spontaneously so.

We can change "personal taste" to "choice," and Bourdieu's words still make sense. Personal opinions, by which he implies personal choices, are socially influenced, constructed, shaped, subjective—whatever you will.

Human beings are social animals. Many of the choices we make are shaped by social considerations, economic ones, and other factors as well. Consider what this site from Harvard University has to say about Bourdieu:

In the course of everyday life, people constantly choose between what they find aesthetically pleasing and what they consider tacky, merely trendy, or ugly. Bourdieu bases his study on surveys that took into account the multitude of social factors that play a part in a French person's choice of clothing, furniture, leisure activities, dinner menus for guests, and many other matters of taste. What emerges from his analysis is that social snobbery is everywhere in the bourgeois world. The different aesthetic choices people make are all distinctions—that is, choices made in opposition to those made by other classes. Taste is not pure. Bourdieu finds a world of social meaning in the decision to order bouillabaisse, in our contemporary cult of thinness, in the "California sports" such as jogging and cross-country skiing. The social world, he argues, functions simultaneously as a system of power relations and as a symbolic system in which minute distinctions of taste become the basis for social judgment.

The topic of Bourdieu's book is a fascinating one: the strategies of social pretension are always curiously engaging. But the book is more than fascinating. It is a major contribution to current debates on the theory of culture and a challenge to the major theoretical schools in contemporary sociology.

Harvard University Press. (n.d.). Harvard University Press Book Catalog.

What we seldom think about is the fact that we are constantly making choices in the course of our everyday lives. Sometimes we turn these choices into habits or routines so we don't have to spend energy in making a choice, but behind the habits or routines, choices lurk.

Case Study: My Morning Breakfast Routine

For example, just about every morning, I start breakfast with a bowl of oatmeal, fortified with chia seeds along with flax seeds, and a glass of hot milk. I chose to have oatmeal rather than several other foods I could eat: grits, cereals such as cornflakes, Wheaties, granola, and so on. I decided I preferred old-fashioned oats zapped for three minutes in my microwave.

Figure 4.2: Oatmeal and Hot Milk

After eating my oatmeal and hot milk, I have half a bagel, toasted, with butter, and a cup of coffee—now an espresso latte, thanks to my espresso machine.

Figure 4.3: Toasted Half Bagel and Latte

Every other day, I also have a soft-boiled egg, boiled for 5:45 minutes. My wife also has oatmeal and part of a bagel, but she prefers tea to coffee. These are our everyday home routines. Deciding on a soft-boiled egg is also a choice since I could have fried eggs, scrambled eggs, poached eggs, and so on.

When my wife and I take cruises, our breakfasts are much more elaborate and often include fruit juice, fruit, yogurt, croissants, toasted English muffins, jam, and so on. We can describe breakfasts on cruise ships as characterized by hyper-baconization. I would guess that many people who don't eat much bacon at home take advantage of the bacon served on cruise ships and have much larger and more complete breakfasts than at home. Others may be used to eating a lot of bacon for breakfast and feast on it while on the ships.

Figure 4.4: Bacon and Two Eggs on the *Royal Princess*

There are many choices for breakfasts on cruise ships and sometimes my wife and I choose bagels and lox, though the bagels on the cruise ships I've sailed on never were real bagels—which means they weren't boiled before being baked. They were really bagel-shaped rolls.

Case Study: Choosing a Home

Choosing a home to purchase is, aside from tuition for many colleges and universities, the biggest purchase/investment most people make. The median price for a house in America (meaning half cost more and half cost less) is $400,000. Many houses, depending upon where one lives, cost much less than that, and there are a surprising number of homes that cost twenty, thirty, or forty million dollars (and up) that multimillionaires and billionaires purchase. Many ultra-rich people have several homes, often in different countries.

When our children were old enough to go to school, my wife and I left San Francisco, which has notoriously poor schools and moved to Mill Valley, five miles north of the Golden Gate Bridge. Mill Valley, like many affluent suburbs or small cities near big cities, has very fine schools.

My wife wanted us to buy a house in a part of Mill Valley near the Old Mill Primary School, but we couldn't find a house we liked or could afford near the Old Mill School, so we purchased a house in a different part of Mill Valley, close to the town's Tamalpais High School. This was in 1970, and I was making $13,000 a year teaching at San Francisco State University. Had I bought a house a year earlier, it would have been a thousand or two thousand dollars less expensive than what I paid for it.

Marin Country, the county in which Mill Valley is located, is one of the hundred most expensive counties in America. There are towns in Marin, such as Belvedere and Ross, where houses cost many millions of dollars, so there is a considerable difference in the cost of one's house depending on where in Marin County one lives. There are even some parts of Marin County where people live in poverty and are homeless.

The inhabitants of Mill Valley now tend to be either people who bought their homes many years ago when they were less expensive (grandfathered in) or, people with very high-paying jobs, such as techies or professionals, or people with prominent positions in corporations or who own successful businesses.

Recently, my wife and I were out for a walk, and a man in a car stopped to talk with us. He had purchased a nearby home owned by a friend of ours who had died and whose wife sold the house. He invited us to come and see what he did with the house, so we walked over to his house, and he showed us around. He had completely transformed the house, and it was really beautiful. He had purchased it for two million dollars and probably spent another million transforming it. He had a wonderful architect who made the most of the house.

The choice of where to live is affected by one's income and many people who would choose to live in Mill Valley can't afford to do so. I will say more about housing later in the book.

The Claritas Typology: Birds of a Feather Flock Together

Research into people's political affiliations suggests we purchase homes in areas where like-minded people in similar socioeconomic classes live. Thus, in many places, most of one's neighbors have the same political party affiliations. So there are blue neighborhoods and red neighborhoods in towns and cities, just as there are blue and red states and some that are purple and moving in one direction or the other.

Marketing companies have developed various typologies of "kinds of consumers" and have found that people in certain zip codes tend to have similar incomes and a similar socioeconomic status. One company, Claritas, identifies some sixty different kinds of consumers and finds, as one might imagine, that those on the top of the list, the most affluent, tend to live near one another. Claritas even has a tool on its website where you can enter your zip code and find out which kinds of consumers live in that zip code. If you go to Claritas 36 Zip Code Lookup, you can find which segments of their typology live in your zip code or any zip code.

My Zip Code, 94941, located in an unincorporated part of Mill Valley, California, has the following Claritas Social Groups:

1 Upper Crust

Wealthy Mature w/o Kids

2 Networked Neighbors

Wealthy Older Mostly w/o Kids

3 Movers & Shakers

Wealthy older Mostly w/o Kids

6 **Winner's Circle**

Wealthy Middle Age Mostly w/ Kids

8 Gray Power

Wealthy Mature w/o Kids

As explained earlier, there are also many people in this Zip Code who have lived here for forty or fifty years and are "grandfathered in," which means if they hadn't bought their homes many years ago, zip code 94941 would be too expensive for them to buy a home. My neighbor, who my wife and I met while we were out for a walk, would probably be classified by Claritas as "Winner's Circle," since he has two kids, is middle-aged, and wealthy. To give you an idea of what the different Claritas lifestyles are, a list of around half of the Claritas Segments, all with jazzy names, is shown below.

01 Upper Crust Wealthy Mature w/o Kids

02 Networked Neighbors Wealthy Middle Age Mostly w/ Kids

03 Movers & Shakers Wealthy Older Mostly w/o Kids

04 Young Digerati Wealthy Younger Mostly w/ Kids

05 Country Squires Wealthy Middle Age Family Mix

06 Winner's Circle Wealthy Middle Age Mostly w/ Kids

07 Money & Brains Wealthy Older Mostly w/o Kids

08 Gray Power Wealthy Mature w/o Kids

09 Big Fish, Small Pond Upscale Mature w/o Kids

10 Executive Suites Upscale Middle Age Mostly w/ Kids

11 Fast-Track Families Upscale Middle Age Family Mix

12 Cruisin' to Retirement Upscale Older Mostly w/o Kids

13 Upward Bound Upscale Younger Family Mix

14 Kids & Cul-de-Sacs Upscale Middle Age Family Mix

15 New Homesteaders Upscale Middle Age Mostly w/ Kids

16 Beltway Boomers Upscale Middle Age Mostly w/o Kids

17 Urban Elders Midscale Older Mostly w/o Kids

18 Mayberry-ville Upscale Older Mostly w/o Kids

19 American Dreams Upper Midscale Middle Age Mostly w/o Kids

20 Empty Nests Upper Midscale Mature w/o Kids

21 The Cosmopolitans Upscale Younger Family Mix

22 Middleburg Managers Upscale Younger Family Mix

23 Township Travelers Upper Midscale Middle Age Family Mix

24 Pickup Patriarchs Upscale Older Mostly w/o Kids

25 Up-and-Comers Upper Midscale Younger Family Mix

26 Home Sweet Home Upper Midscale Older w/o Kids

27 Big Sky Families Upscale Middle Age Mostly w/ Kids

28 Country Casuals Upper Midscale Older Mostly w/o Kids

29 White Picket Fences Midscale Middle Age Family Mix

30 Pools & Patios Upper Midscale Younger Mostly w/ Kids

31 Connected Bohemians Midscale Younger Mostly w/o Kids

32 Traditional Times Upper Midscale Mature w/o Kids

PRIZM® Premier P$YCLE® Premier ConneXions® (https://www.claritas.com) 1-888-981-4 1 888 981 4 CONTACT US

Claritas argues that its list of lifestyles enables marketing directors and advertising agencies to focus their attention on the right target audiences and not waste money trying to sell things to people who either wouldn't be interested in what was being advertised or couldn't afford the products and services being advertised.

Readers of this book can find themselves in this list of lifestyles and can go to Claritas, put in their Zip Codes, and find which lifestyles are prevalent where they live. My wife and I probably belong to the lifestyle "20: Empty Nests Upper Midscale Mature w/o Kids."

Claritas and other such firms have developed typologies that list groups of consumers based on their lifestyles. These typologies suggest that people's choices are shaped by the groups to which they belong, even though individuals making their choices may not be aware of the extent to which their groups, of one kind or another, shape their behavior.

Figure 4.5: Emile Durkheim

The great French sociologist Emile Durkheim explained that the relationship that exists between individuals and society is complex. He wrote that man (and now we would add woman) exists in society, as an individual, but also that society exists in individuals, shaping their thinking and behavior. This means society has an impact on our choices even if we do not recognize this matter.

Emile Durkheim, a prominent sociologist of the late nineteenth and early twentieth centuries, focused his research on understanding the role of social forces in shaping individual behavior and society as a whole. While he did not extensively write about choices in the same way that contemporary psychologists or decision theorists do, his work provides insights into how social factors influence the choices individuals make.

Durkheim argued that individuals are not isolated beings but products of their social environment. He believed that social facts, which are external to individuals and exert coercive power over them, play a crucial role in shaping human behavior, including the choices they make. According to Durkheim, these social facts include social norms, values, beliefs, and institutions that are present in a society.

Durkheim emphasized the importance of collective consciousness, which refers to the shared beliefs, values, and moral attitudes that bind individuals together in a society. He argued that collective consciousness exerts a powerful influence on individuals' choices by shaping their perceptions of right and wrong, acceptable and unacceptable behaviors, and their sense of moral obligation.

Furthermore, Durkheim highlighted the concept of social integration or cohesion. He believed that individuals' level of integration within society affects their choices and behavior. When individuals feel connected to and supported by their social groups, they are more likely to conform to the norms and values of the group, influencing their decision-making processes.

Durkheim also explored the relationship between individual freedom and social constraints. He acknowledged that individuals have personal desires and preferences, but he emphasized that these must be balanced with the needs and expectations of the larger social group. According to Durkheim, too much individual freedom without social regulation could lead to anomie—a state of normlessness and social disintegration—while excessive social constraint could stifle individual autonomy and creativity.

In summary, Durkheim's perspective on choices can be understood within the broader framework of his sociological theories. He emphasized the influence of social facts, collective consciousness, social integration, and the balance between individual freedom and social constraint on the choices individuals make. According to Durkheim, understanding the social context and its impact on individuals is essential for comprehending the choices they make and their behavior within society.

We can think about choices in terms of their effects on our lives. Some choices we make are extremely important, others are less important, and some are relatively trivial. Let me offer a typology of choices we all make in our lives.

Occupations

Since most people work for many years, their choice of occupation (if they can choose what kind of work to do) is of pivotal importance. One's income shapes many other choices people make. If you have a job that pays well, your ability to make other choices is greatly enhanced. For many people, their occupation is a major aspect of their identity.

Marriage or non-marriage

Most people get married, though a large proportion of these marriages end in divorce, which suggests that the choice of a marriage partner was a poor one. Married people (or people living together) spend a lot of time with their partners, so one's marriage choice is an important part of one's identity. Divorce can be seen as a form of "buyer's remorse."

Education

Education is a key aspect of social mobility, so the amount of education one receives is all-important in terms of one's ability to make choices as far as occupations, spouses, homes, and many other matters. The kind of education one receives, and the amount of education are both important. As far as identity is concerned, the prestige of the colleges or universities one attends is significant.

Those who attend Ivy League schools or other selective schools are validated for the rest of their lives by having graduated from these institutions. Some of my friends who have graduated from elite universities do not fail to mention their schools in conversations fifty years after having attended them.

Home and location

Our homes, as pointed out earlier, are the most expensive purchases we make, so the kind of homes we buy and their location play an important role in our lives.

My wife and I spent five years living in San Francisco, but when it came time for our children to go to school, we moved to Mill Valley, which has an excellent school system. This behavior is typical of many families who (if they can afford to do so) move from urban locations to suburbs, where the schools are better, and the quality of life is more to their liking.

Automobiles

The automobiles we purchase are one of our largest expenses and are conventionally understood to be signifiers of our socio-economic status and taste. People with many children generally find themselves purchasing cars that can hold many people, so our automobile choices are affected by our need to choose certain models of cars. When ferrying children is not a major consideration in choosing cars, then choice becomes more personal, but our income determines whether the cars we like are the cars we choose. Our taste may be for a Porsche, but our income forces us to purchase a Honda Civic or Toyota Corolla.

Religion

Many people remain with the religion of their parents, but it is possible to change religions. Our religions, depending upon their nature, can play a major role in many of the things we do, including the foods we eat, our daily lives, our entertainment, and so on. Conservative religions, such as Mormonism,

Catholicism, and Orthodox Judaism, play a much larger role in our daily lives than liberal ones.

Political affiliations

Aristotle said that man is a "political animal," and if you understand politics in its broadest sense, we can see that one's politics and party identification are now increasingly important as America divides into antagonistic red and blue towns, cities, and states. We now find that where people live is often shaped by political considerations, and conservatives like to live in areas with many other conservatives.

Aristotle on Choices

Here is a discussion of Aristotle's ideas about choices from the New World Encyclopedia:

> While Aristotle inherits many of the basic Platonic ideas, he analyzes the notion of choice in a less ideal and more concrete or experiential manner. Like Plato, Aristotle views choice in relation to the end or good of all our actions, which he defines as "eudemonia" or happiness. The attainment of happiness depends upon the acquisition of specific virtues which are attained through practice and which enable the human being to function in its proper way or nature. He defines choice as a "deliberate appetition" which involves a dispositional directedness toward some end (a good or apparent good) and the rational deliberation of how to achieve that end. That is, one deliberates over the best means to achieve some specific end or good out of the various possibilities or options. Aristotle considered choice to be a "practical syllogism" in that the major premise is the desired goal, good, or end, the minor premise is the rational deliberation of the best means to achieve it, which involves a kind of working one's way backward from the goal that one seeks to the necessary steps to achieve it. Finally, the conclusion of the syllogism is not merely the theoretical idea of what one must do to achieve the goal, but the performing of the first action or choice necessary to achieving it.

> New World Encyclopedia. (n.d.). "Choice."

With Aristotle's ideas in mind, we can turn our attention to the subject of everyday choices, which is a major concern in this book.

Everyday Life Choices

There are any number of everyday life choices we make, several of which will be discussed in various places in this book:

Clothes

Food preferences

Home furnishings

Electronic devices

Hobbies

Smartphones

Objects of all kinds

Movies (genres)

Television shows

Music

Sports

Ad infinitum

When it comes to choices, Americans, thanks to the power of our advertising industry, have enormous knowledge of consumer products, even if they may know relatively little about politics or other matters.

The import of semiotics in the study of brands has been proliferating over the past twenty years from academics and practitioners alike. By virtue of semiotics' ability to account for the processes whereby meaning is generated, it constitutes the discipline par excellence for addressing the issue of brand signification. Semiotic approaches to branding have been furnished both from within the semiotics (e.g., Floch, Semprini, Rossolatos) and the consumer research (e.g., Mick & McQuarrie, Stern, Williamson) disciplines. Semiotic approaches have been incumbent on different perspectives in semiotic literature, such as Peirceanism, Structuralism, and Social Semiotics. Semiotics has been applied in various marketing-related research areas, including strategic brand positioning, brand identity, brand equity and brand image, advertising copy development, advertising encoding and decoding, retail branding, media messages, and package design, to name a few. The usefulness of semiotics consists both in furnishing typologies of brands as signs, as well as a conceptual and methodological platform for designing and managing brands as sign systems. As an applied market research tool, semiotics has been used either as a standalone research method or in combination with other qualitative and quantitative research techniques. Semiotic concepts have been used in order to single and map out cultural codes, product languages, consumer typologies, alternative communication, and packaging routes.

International Association for Semiotic Studies. (n.d). "Import of Semiotics in the Study of Brands." *International Journal of Marketing Semiotics.* iass-ais.org/cfp-international-journal-of-marketing-semiotics/

Since the meaning of a sign depends on the code within which it is situated, codes provide a framework within which signs make sense. Indeed, we cannot grant something the status of a sign if it does not function within a code....The conventions of codes represent a social dimension in semiotics: a code is a set of practices familiar to users of the medium operating with a broad cultural framework....When studying cultural practices, semioticians treat as signs any objects or actions which have meaning to the members of a cultural group, seeking to identify the rules or conventions of the codes which underlie the production of meaning within that culture.

Daniel Chandler. 2002. *Semiotics: The Basics.*

Chapter 5
The Semiotics of Choice

Semiotics is commonly described as the science of signs, a sign being anything that generates meaning and can stand for something else, whether that something else exists or not.

> Signs are used to communicate meanings between individuals. An individual constructs a message in his mind, a complex meaning, an idea or thought process, which he wishes to convey to someone else. Both individuals possess a common code or grammar which they have learned. An individual constructs a message in his mind….It is picked up by the second individual, the receiver, who then decodes the signal and thus obtains the original message. An idea has been transferred from one mind to another.

> Peter Wollen. 1969. *Signs and Meaning in the Cinema.*

A sociologist who uses semiotics, Mark Gottdiener, offers another explanation of semiotics:

> The basic unit of semiotics is the *sign* defined conceptually as something that stands for something else, and, more technically, as a spoken or written word, a drawn figure, or a material object unified in the mind with a particular cultural concept. The sign is this unity of word-object, known as a *signifier* with a corresponding, culturally prescribed content or meaning, known as a *signified*. Thus, our minds attach the word "dog," or the drawn figure of a "dog," as a signifier to the idea of a "dog," that is, a domesticated canine species possessing certain behavioral characteristics. If we came from a culture that did not possess dogs in daily life, however unlikely, we would not know what the signifier "dog" means….When dealing with objects that are signifiers of certain concepts, cultural meanings, or ideologies of belief, we can consider them not only as "signs," but *sign vehicles*. (p. 8, 9)

> Mark Gottdiener. 1997. *The Theming of America: Dream, Visions and Commercial Spaces*

As Daniel Chandler, author of a widely read book on semiotics, explains in the epigraph, you must know the codes in your culture to understand what signs mean, and growing up in a culture means being imprinted with the codes of that culture. Since the meaning of signs changes, we must be on guard and make sure we don't misinterpret signs.

Figure 5.1: Ferdinand de Saussure

Ferdinand de Saussure, one of the founding fathers of semiotics (though he called his theory semiology, or words about signs) explained that signs have two parts: a sound or object or image, which he called a *signifier* and the message or meaning of that signifier, which he called a *signified.*

Since the meaning of signs can change, a given signifier can, when changes occur, generate a different signified.

He writes in his book (1965, 67):

> I call the combination of a concept and a sound-image a *sign.*....I propose to retain the world sign [*sign*] to designate the whole and to replace *concept* and *sound-image* respectively by *signified* [*signifié*] and *signifier* [signifiant]; the last two terms have the advantage of indicating the opposition that separates them from each other and from the whole of which they are parts.

Saussure used a diagram, shown below, to suggest the relationship that exists between signifiers and signifieds.

Figure 5.2: Signifier/Signified. Berger, after Saussure

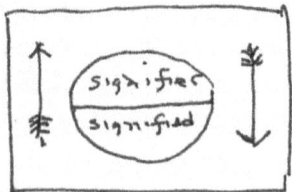

For example, long hair on men, many years ago, signified artist or musician, but now it is so common that it has lost its original meaning.

Maya Pines, a journalist, offers an insight into semiotics when she explains that signs are messages and we are always sending messages about ourselves and receiving messages from others, even if we are not aware of doing so. She writes:

> Everything we do sends messages about us in a variety of codes, semiologists contend. We are also on the receiving end of innumerable messages encoded in music, gestures, foods, rituals, books, movies, or advertisements. Yet we seldom realize that we have received such messages and would have trouble explaining the rules under which they operate.
>
> Maya Pines. October 13, 1982. "How They Know What You Really Mean." *San Francisco Chronicle.*

Sometimes, we don't send the messages we think we are sending, and sometimes, others don't interpret the messages we are sending correctly—that is, the way we intended them to be interpreted.

An Italian novelist and semiotician, Umberto Eco, argued that most people don't interpret the messages they receive correctly—the way the sender of the messages expected them to be interpreted. He called this "aberrant decoding." Semioticians suggest that "aberrant decoding" by receivers of messages occurs in a large percentage of the population.

Figure 5.3: Charles Sanders Peirce

The other founding father of semiotics, Charles Sanders Peirce, a Harvard philosopher, who gave the science its name, semiotics, explained that there are three kinds of signs: icons, indexes, and symbols.

Peirce suggested some signs work by resemblance. He called them icons. Other kinds of signs work based on cause and effect. If you see smoke billowing out of the window of a house, you can infer that the house is on fire. He called them indexical signs. And with some signs, what Peirce called symbols, you must learn their meaning. You must learn, for example, that a cross is a symbol of Christianity, and an aleph is a Hebrew letter.

Figure 5.4: Aleph

Table 5.1: Peirce's icon/index/symbol

Sign	Icon	Index	Symbol
Signify By	Resemblance	Causal Connection	Must Learn
Examples	Photograph	Smoke signifies fire	Aleph is a Hebrew Letter
Process	Can see	Can Reason	Must Learn

Table by the Author

Semiotics has important things to say about communications of all kinds, but it is especially useful in understanding visual communication and the choices we make in everything from espresso machines, spouses, homes, automobiles, and many other things. If we have a certain amount of money to purchase something, often the way it looks plays an important role. There are commercial semioticians who advise companies and advertising agencies about exploiting how things look for their products and services to shape people's choices and making sure their messages will be interpreted as correctly as possible.

The Branded Self

Brands play a major role in the choices we make for everything from strawberries (and other foods) to suits and dresses (and most of the things we wear and buy.) I have suggested in many of my writings that people's sense of themselves is shaped by the brands they choose.

Brands use advertising to establish an aura and to suggest to consumers what kinds of people favor their brand. Technically, brands use icons to identify themselves and to distinguish themselves both from other brands and from non-branded generic competitors and products. We see the battle between brands played out everywhere—in the media and in our everyday experiences, such as shopping in a supermarket. Commercials enable brands to establish their personas, which helps consumers make choices.

Upscale brands signify status, success, and wealth and provide people with a sense of importance. Consumers also must consider matters like models of brands. Thus, there are many models of most automobile brands, from entry-level cars to top of the line cars. And we can say the same for many other products, such as smart watches, smart phones, blue jeans, ad infinitum.

We brand ourselves and use these brands to both secure an identity and project an identity to others. In *Marketing for Hospitality Tourism* (2nd Edition) by Philip Kotler, John Bowen, and James Makens, we find a classic definition of brands (1999, 284):

> A *brand* is a name, term, sign, symbol, design, or a combination of these elements that is intended to identify the goods or services of a seller and differentiate them from those of competitors. A brand name is the part of the brand that can be vocalized…a brand mark is that part of the brand that can be recognized but is not utterable, such as a symbol, design, or distinctive coloring or lettering. A brand is a sign, and a sign is anything that can be used to stand for something else. Examples are McDonald's Golden Arches and Hilton's H. A trademark is a brand or part of a brand that is given legal protection; it protects the seller's exclusive right to use the brand name or brand mark.

Many scholars have expanded our understanding of brands to suggest they not only are signs and symbols that identify goods and services but also brands are a major factor in the identities of corporations that use brands.

Branding involves differentiation between products and services. But, as Anthony Cortese explains in his book, the differences between products are often trivial, and it is advertising and branding that must find a way to suggest they are different. He writes, in his book *Provocateur: Images of Women and Minorities in Advertising* (1999, 4):

> Branding seeks to nullify or compensate for the fact that products are otherwise fundamentally interchangeable. Tests have shown that consumers cannot distinguish their own brand of soap, beer, cigarette, water, cola, shampoo, gasoline from others. In a sense, advertising is like holding up two identical photographs and persuading you that they are different—in fact, that one is better than the other.

This persuasion is done through linguistic devices such as metaphor and metonymy, images, dramatic narratives we call commercials and any other means that marketers and advertisers can devise to convince us to choose one brand of a product over another.

Metaphors, linguists explain, communicate by analogy, while metonymy communicates by association. It turns out that much of our thinking is based on metaphor and metonymy, and weaker forms of each, simile and synecdoche. These linguistic devices are used all the time in advertising to create emotional responses to brands that are being advertised and shape our choices as consumers. The chart below offers us an understanding of these forms of communication:

Table 5.2: Metaphor and Metonymy

Metaphor	Metonymy
My love is a red rose	The color red is associated with passion, love. Rolls Royce associated with wealth
Simile	**Synecdoche**
My love *is like* a red rose Uses "is like" or "as"	Pentagon stands for American military. (A part stands for the whole or vice versa)

Table by the Author

Metaphor and metonymy play a much more important role in our lives than we imagine. As George Lakoff and Mark Johnson point out in their book, *Metaphors We Live By* (1980, 3):

> Most people think they can get along perfectly well without metaphor. We have found, on the contrary, that metaphor is pervasive in everyday life, not just in language, but in thought and action. Our ordinary conceptual system, in terms of which we both think and act, is fundamentally metaphoric in nature. The concepts that govern our thought are not just matters of intellect. They also govern our everyday functioning down to the most mundane details. Our concepts structure what we perceive, how we get around in the world, and how we relate to other people. Our conceptual system thus plays a central role in defining our everyday realities.

Metaphors and metonymy shape much of our thinking and communication, shaping our everyday thinking—even if we don't recognize that this is the case or assume that metaphor and metonymy are merely literary devices. These devices pervade our everyday speech. Advertisers and marketers use them all the time to communicate with target audiences and shape, as best they can, their thinking.

Brands are what semioticians describe as signifiers (and what Peirce calls icons) that companies use to establish their identities. As pointed out earlier, the essence of a brand is being "different" from other brands and from generic products.

This Fidji perfume advertisement is full of interesting signs that have an emotional impact on those who see it. The snake suggests the Garden of Eden. The flower is a sexual symbol, and the woman holds the bottle in a curious way. If you see the snake as an "s" and the horizontal lines of the bottle as forming an "E," the fingers form an "X" which means there is a sexual dimension to this advertisement that is hidden in its design. We can say the same for many print advertisements and commercials.

Figure 5.5: Fidji perfume advertisement

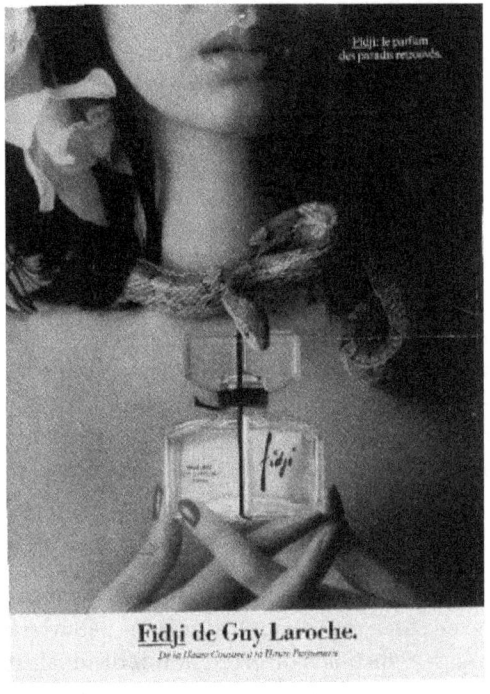

Advertising is what companies use to generate an image of what kinds of people use their products. From a Saussurean perspective, we can say, "in brands, there are only differences." Brands compete with one another and with generic products or commodities.

Laura R. Oswald's article, "Semiotics and Strategic Brand Management," discusses the role of semiotics in creating brands:

> Over the past ten years or so, brand strategy researchers have come to recognize the importance of brand communication in building and sustaining brand equity, the value attached to a brand name or log that supersedes product attributes and differentiates brands in the competitive arena.... The contribution of brand meanings and perceptions to profitability—the Coca-Cola brand is valued at over $70 billion—testifies to the power of symbolic representation to capture the hearts and minds of consumers by means of visual, audio, and verbal signs. The semiotic—or symbolic—dimension of brands is therefore instrumental for building awareness, positive associations, and long-

term customer loyalty, and contributes to trademark ownership and operational advantages such as channel and media clout. Consequently, managing brand equity means managing brand **semiotics.**

Laura Oswald. 2007. "Semiotics and Strategic Brand Management."

Semiotic theory, more than anything else, she argues, enables us to understand what brands are, how they work, and the role they play in consumer decision-making.

Branding claims distinctiveness—relative to other brands that is. It is advertising, more than anything else, that brands use to establish their identities and to portray the kind of people who use, or should use, that brand. Some brands use celebrities in their advertising. In other cases, a celebrity or prominent person wears a product that becomes popular.

When we see a person wearing a certain brand of clothing or a collection of brands, we get, we believe, a sense of what the person using the brands is like—if that is, we have seen advertisements for the brand and know something about it. Branded luxury objects are status symbols and help confer high status upon those who use them.

In his book, *Marketing in Context: Setting the Scene,* Chris Hackley, a professor of marketing, offers some insights about marketing and choice (2013, 163-164):

> Marketing, as a field that embraces the full context of consumer culture, can be conceived, then, as an applied arm of behavioral science. Its appeal to the basest instincts or greed and individualism gives it the purest integrity as a testing bed for behavioral interventions. Whatever people may feel about marketing, this is the sharp edge, and humans respond to marketing without coercion or compunction. We respond because we like it. When we are eating fatty fast food, drinking sugar-loaded drinks, voting for our favored political party, or choosing a new car or TV set, we may face the massive promotional resources of global corporations telling us what our happy lifestyle should look like, but in the end, we are free to choose. True, the choice might be delimited in concentrated market structure, but is nonetheless a choice. Marketing gives us a rich resource of symbols with which we can play in our experiments around identity, fantasy, authenticity, and sheer hedonism.

Hackley suggests that despite the power of marketing, people are still "free to choose" in their quest to establish an identity. This is important to keep in mind. Why people choose the way they do is the subject of the next chapter.

Psychoanalytic theory postulates a multitude of different change mechanisms, and a host of new ways of conceptualizing the change process continue to emerge as psychoanalytic theories themselves evolve and proliferate. At the most basic level, there is an understanding that change generally involves making the unconscious conscious, as expressed by Freud's oft cited axiom: "Where id has been there shall ego be." Although Freud's understanding of the nature of the change process evolved over the course of his lifetime, central to his mature thinking was the idea that change involves first becoming aware of our instinctual impulses and unconscious wishes, and then learning to deal with them in a mature, rational, and reflective fashion. For Freud, a central premise was thus that we are driven by unconscious wishes that we are unaware of and this lack of awareness results in driven or self-defeating behavior. Freud believed we delude ourselves about reasons for our behaviors and this self-deception limits our choice. By becoming aware of our unconscious wishes and our defenses against them we increase the choices available to us. Thus, as we decrease the extent to which we are driven by unconscious factors, we assume a greater degree of agency.

J.D. Safran, E. Gardner-Schuster. 2016. In *Encyclopedia of Mental Health (Second Edition)*.

We may say that the id comprises the psychic representatives of the drives, the ego consists of those functions that have to do with the individual's relation to his environment, and the superego comprises the moral precepts of our minds as well as our ideal aspirations. The drives, of course, we assume to be present from birth, but the same is certainly not true of interest in or control of the environment on the one hand nor of any moral sense or aspirations on the other. It is obvious that neither of the latter, that is, neither the ego nor the superego, develops till sometime after birth. Freud expressed this fact by assuming that the id comprised the entire psychic apparatus at birth, and that the ego and superego were originally parts of the id, which differentiated sufficiently in the course of growth to warrant their being considered as separate functional entities.

Charles Brenner. 1974. *An Elementary Textbook of Psychoanalysis.*

Chapter 6

Choice and the Psyche

This chapter uses classical Freudian psychoanalytic theory to explore the psychological dimensions of choice. Let us recall that people, according to some thinkers, are free to act as they choose but not free to choose as they choose, which means they have the illusion that their choices are personal and based on phenomena such as fads and taste.

Figure 6.1: Sigmund Freud

Sigmund Freud, the founding father of psychoanalytic theory, suggested that the psyche has three levels: consciousness, the subconscious or preconscious, and the unconscious.

As Freud explained in "One of the Difficulties of Psychoanalysis." (1910/1963b):

> You believe that you are informed of all that goes on in your mind if it is of any importance at all, because your consciousness then gives news of it. And if you have heard nothing of any particular thing in your mind you confidently assume that it does not exist there. Indeed, you go so far as to regard "the mind" as coextensive with "consciousness," that is, with what is known to you….[what you are] conscious of; whether something is going on in your mind and whether you hear of it, are two different things.

It is useful to suggest that the levels of consciousness can be represented by an iceberg, which is shown in the drawing that follows. Technically, this drawing is based on the device of simile, a weak form of metaphor that uses the notion that something is like something else.

Figure 6.2: Representation of Consciousness, Subconsciousness and Unconsciousness

We can see the tip of the iceberg, which represents consciousness. Just below the waterline, we can dimly make out the iceberg, which represents the preconscious or subconscious. And below the preconscious, representing the major part of the psyche, which we cannot access or know without the help of psychologists, psychoanalysts, psychiatrists, and other kinds of professionals, is the unconscious.

Tapping into unconscious feelings and notions in target audiences is a central interest to companies that produce products and services to sell and to the marketers and advertising agencies that work for them.

It is important to recognize that the unrecognized imperatives in the unconscious shape much of our thinking and behavior, including the choices we make in a wide variety of areas. In the epilogue of this chapter, the author explains that if we can become aware of the forces in our unconscious, we can make better choices.

A more contemporary figure, Gerald Zaltman, a professor of marketing at the Harvard Business School, is also interested in choices and the psyche and suggests that the unconscious plays an important role in our purchasing decisions. He writes, in his book, *How Customers Think: Essential Insights into the Mind of the Market* (2003, 50):

> At least 95 percent of all cognition occurs below awareness in the shadows of the mind while, at most, only 5 percent occurs in high order consciousness.

Were Zalman to draw an iceberg representing the psyche, the amount of the iceberg appearing above the water would be much smaller than what is shown in my drawing of the iceberg.

Zaltman explains that metaphors play an important role in the way we think about things and writes (2003, 37-38):

> Metaphors stimulate the workings of the human mind. By one estimate, we use almost six metaphors per minute of spoken language....Speaking

metaphorically, metaphor is the engine of imagination....Metaphors can help bring consumers important—but unconscious—thoughts and feelings to the surface. Indeed, metaphor constitutes a powerful tool for unearthing the hidden thoughts and feelings that have such a profound influence on consumers' decision making.

The decision-making of consumers is, let me suggest, another way of indicating the choices they make.

What is important is to recognize that the behavior of consumers is not completely rational, and many choices consumers make are affected in important ways by thoughts, ideas, and feelings of which they are unaware but which play an important role in our decision-making/choosing in many areas.

These three levels of mind or psyche are known as Freud's topographic hypothesis, topography being defined as relating to the physical features of an area. Freud also developed another hypothesis, his structural hypothesis, which deals with three components of the psyche that are in complicated relationships with one another—the id, the ego, and the superego.

Figure 6.3: The Id, Ego and Superego.

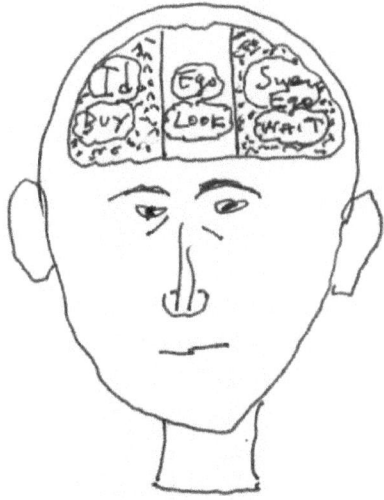

A psychoanalyst, Charles Brenner, offers a brief description of these three entities in his book, *An Elementary Textbook of Psychoanalysis: Revised and Expanded Edition* (1974, 35):

We may say that the id comprises the psychic representatives of the drives, the ego consists of those functions which have to do with the individual's relation to his environment, and the superego comprises the moral precepts of our minds as well as our ideal aspirations.

Freud offers a description of the id that gives us an idea of what it is like. He writes, in his *New Introductory Lectures on Psychoanalysis* (quoted in Hinsie & Campbell, 1970, 372):

> We can come nearer to the id with images, and call it chaos, a cauldron of seething excitement. We suppose that it is somewhere in direct contact with somatic processes and takes over from them instinctual needs and gives them mental expression, but we cannot say in what substratum this contact is made. These instincts fill it with energy, but it has no organization, and no unified will, only an impulsion to obtain satisfaction for the instinctual needs, in accordance with the pleasure principle.

We cannot allow this seething cauldron of sexual desire, passion, and lust to determine our actions because we are social animals who live in societies, and civilization demands that we find ways to control our behavior. In fact, the demands that civilization makes on us are so great, according to Freud in his book *Civilization and Its Discontents,* that we all suffer from great psychological pressure and pain. Much of this is caused by the superego.

The superego corresponds, as Brenner (1974, 111-112) notes, "in a general way to what we ordinarily call conscience. It comprises the moral functions of the personality."

The image from the United Airlines advertisement below offers the following list of Id and Superego differences. I offer this list because it is difficult to read the items in the image:

The ID	The Superego
Crave Dom Perignon	Better get to work
Long for good movie	Better call the office
Thirst for Mozart on CD	Better call the client
Covet caviar canape	Better write the brief
Yearn for filet mignon	Better make the brief better

This advertisement uses humor to attract the attention of readers who may be looking for an airline to fly somewhere. Notice that the id items are all upscale and expensive, which suggests the advertisement may be directed to people with sophisticated tastes and high-paying jobs.

Figure 6.4: Detail from United Airlines Advertisement

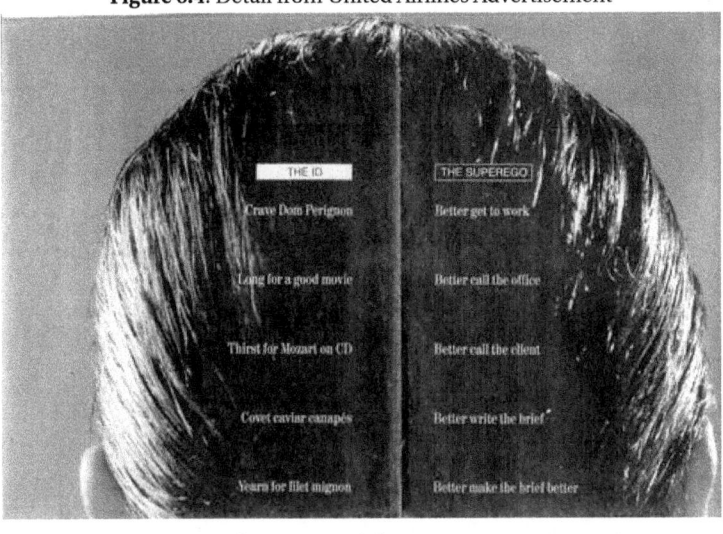

Brenner lists the primary functions of the superego (1974, 112):

1. the approval or disapproval of actions and wishes on the grounds of rectitude. 2. critical self-observation. 3. self-punishment. 4. the demand for reparation or repentance of wrong-doing. 5. self-praise or self-love as a reward for virtuous or desirable thoughts and actions. Contrary to the ordinary meaning of "conscience," however, we understand that the functions of the superego are often largely or completely unconscious.

There is an endless but unconscious battle that exists between the id and the superego. The ego tries to mediate between them, operating always with the aim of self-preservation. The ego carries out its function by storing experiences in the memory, avoiding excessively powerful stimuli through flight, adapting to moderately strong stimuli, and bringing about changes in the world through activity.

We can suggest the relationship among these elements involving choice.

Table 6.1: Id, Ego and Superego

ID	EGO	SUPEREGO
Desire for Things	Restraint	Attacks Desires
Emotion	Logic	Guilt
Lust	Reason	Anxiety
	Table by the Author	

Many of what we may describe as desire for things stem from emotional responses made by the Id. The Ego tries to moderate these desires while the Superego, which is based on guilt, tries to restrain the behavior of the Id.

If we were to push this to extremes, the Id elements in our psyches would choose to buy everything that attracts our attention, the Ego would plead for moderation based on things like their cost and the Superego would feel guilty about all of the Id's choices and desires.

Advertising, we can add, focuses on Id elements in our psyches and tries to avoid stimulating the Superego. We can use Freud's typology to understand the appeal of books, films, television shows, and even cities.

Below, I provide some examples of what happens when we apply Freud's Id/Ego/Superego typology to culture, in general.

Table 6.2: Id, Ego and Superego and Culture

TOPIC	ID	EGO	SUPEREGO
Book genres	Romances	Textbooks	Bible, Koran
Cities	Las Vegas	Boston	Vatican City
Heroes	Don Juan	Sherlock Holmes	Superman
TV shows	Dancing with Stars	Nature, Nova	Religious Shows

Table by the Author

Freud also wrote about defense mechanisms that the Ego uses to deal with anxieties people feel. Some of the defense mechanisms related to choices and consumer culture follow: ambivalence, fixation, rationalization, and buyer's regrets.

Ambivalence

A simultaneous feeling of love and hate for some person or object, which can affect choices people have made and changes they might make.

Fixation

An obsessive attraction to someone or something often the result of a traumatic experience. We can use this concept to understand the passion people feel about purchasing some product or service.

Rationalization

Offering logical reasons for behavior generated by unconscious and irrational determinants or choices, often used by people who make irrational purchases or do irrational things.

Buyer's Remorse

There is another psychological phenomenon related to our choices of things we purchase, namely buyer's remorse. It is often the case that someone purchases some product or service and, after buying it, either experiences a sense of regret because it doesn't work as well as expected, or is thought to be too expensive. The buyers conclude that they should have waited for a better deal or chosen a different brand or model of what they purchased and were disappointed. I see this phenomenon as basically connected with the Superego and diffuse feelings of guilt for having made a "bad" choice.

Psychology Today offers some ideas on Buyer's Remorse

> Although the notion of buyer's remorse is familiar to most of us and in our personal experience may feel common, social science research reveals that we are actually psychologically motivated to be satisfied with our decisions. On the simplest level, if our choices are informed by trustworthy data, we increase the chances of good outcomes. That's why we hear parents and teachers emphasizing to kids the importance of "making good decisions." But beyond that, psychological processes, frequently active without our awareness, promote decision satisfaction. According to a well-known theory, cognitive dissonance arises when an individual experiences psychologically inconsistent (dissonant) thoughts (cognitions). For example, the cognition "I am a competent decision maker" is inconsistent with the cognition "I made a bad decision." Cognitive dissonance is psychologically uncomfortable. And that discomfort motivates the individual to mitigate that discomfort. To reduce the dissonance a person might decide that the decision isn't so bad, that alternative choices would have created worse consequences, that the good consequences of the choice are so good that they far outweigh its bad aspects. Such dissonance reduction usually cancels out or moderates feelings of buyer's remorse. Sometimes it leads us to repurpose our buyer's remorse for defensive purposes. For example, if you can avoid responsibility for the decision ("I was lied to or cheated," or "Anyone would have made the same choice."), a bad decision can be reconciled to your belief that you are a good decision maker.

> These psychological processes are internal. They take place even if no one else is privy to our thoughts. Often, of course, we have to contend with making our private cognitions public. That is, our concerns about self-presentation can influence the tension between cognitive dissonance and buyer's remorse.

> Harold Sigall. 2017, August 17. "Buyer's remorse." *Psychology Today.*

Frequently, when people think about purchasing something, they become very excited about what they will be buying and even fixated on it, only to be consumed by a sense of disappointment when they actually have the product or service they chose.

We see examples of buyer's remorse in the many negative comments people make in their evaluation of products shown on Amazon.com's pages of responses of buyers for various products they purchased, in the negative comments people who write about their cruises on websites such as Cruise Critic, or in the comments members of the Home Espresso Aficionados as they write, endlessly it seems, about their desire to purchase better and more expensive espresso machines and grinders. These new and more expensive espresso machines and grinders are, indirectly, manifestations of buyer's remorse or regret.

It is interesting to note that many of the negative comments people write about their cruises are countered by positive assessments by other passengers on the same cruise, which leads us to recognize that people who evaluate cruises and other purchases tend to be either very negative or very positive and that most passengers are satisfied and don't bother to review their cruises.

Figure 6.5: Joan Riviere

Joan Riviere offers an insight into what motivates people to desire and choose to purchase objects and services. She writes, in "Hate, Greed and Aggression," her contribution to a book co-authored with Melanie Klein, *Love, Hate and Reparation* (1934/1967, 26-207):

> Some measure of greed exists unconsciously in everyone. It represents an aspect of the desire to live, one which is mingled and fused at the outset of life with the impulse to turn aggression and destructiveness outside ourselves against others, and as such it persists unconsciously throughout life. By its very nature it is endless and never assuaged; and being a form of the impulse to live, it ceases only with death.

The longing or greed for good things can relate to any and every imaginable kind of good--material possessions, bodily or mental gifts, advantages and privileges; but, beside the actual gratifications they may bring, in the depths of our minds, they ultimately signify one thing. They stand as proof to us, if we get them, that we are ourselves good, and full of good, and so are worthy of love, or respect and honour, in return. Thus, they serve as proof and insurances against our fears of emptiness inside ourselves, or of our evil impulses, which make us feel bad and full of badness to ourselves and others.

Motivating our choices, in the final analysis, is a desire to demonstrate that we are good and worthy of love and respect. How we do that, as we negotiate the endless variety of goods and services from which we can choose, is a complicated matter, but these imperatives, we can suggest, are lodged in our unconscious and difficult for us to fully understand or recognize.

PART TWO:
APPLICATIONS

Shakespeare's definition of love can be identified in the themes of mortality and physical affection, which are sprinkled throughout nearly all of Shakespeare's sonnets. According to "*The Norton Anthology of English Literature,*" Shakespeare's sonnets, particularly "the subsequent long sequence (18 to 126) ... develops as a dominant motif the transience and destructive power of time, countered only by the force of love...." (Greenblatt, 540). Throughout these sonnets, a "destructive power of time" and the inevitability of age and death are clearly evident and easily identified. However, this emphasis on the fleetingness of time is intertwined with the mortality of love. Love, for Shakespeare, as exemplified in his sonnets, was simply an output of human affection, doomed to perish along with those who hold endearment to high importance. To begin on the first part of the contrived definition, it is necessary to understand the themes of beauty illustrated and expounded upon by Shakespeare. In the first sonnet, the author begins with the following lines describing beauty: "From fairest creatures we desire increase, that thereby beauty's rose might never die, but as the riper should by time decease, His tender heir might bear his memory...." Here, Shakespeare begins speaking of the allure of humans, a matter that he may find to be an excessively important factor in love and loving, as outward beauty is oftentimes an initial foreground for immediate connections, and sometimes, relationships. Shakespeare then stresses the importance of continuing such beauty through reproduction, as evidenced by "from fairest creatures we desire increase."

Katherine Blanner. 2016, January 18. "Shakespeare's definition of love." *The Odyssey Online.*

Although there isn't one clear definition, romantic love is most often thought of as a combination of attraction and idealization that can result in (or from) a bonded relationship. Romantic love has inspired artists for centuries and been the subject of countless plays, songs, movies, books, and other creative endeavors. As anyone who's been in love knows, love is complicated and capable of eliciting strong emotions, from elation to heartbreak. Romantic relationships go through ups and downs—from that initial, intoxicating "honeymoon" phase to a sense of disappointment and, ideally, to a state of acceptance and a desire for permanence. It can be challenging to move through these phases, but the reward is a healthy, long-term relationship.

Sheri Stritof. 2022, March 30. "What is romantic love?" *Verywell Mind.*

Chapter 7

Choosing a Partner

Marlene Dietrich sang a song that tells us a great deal about the nature of love, which we can assume is a basic factor in choosing a partner. She sings about falling in love again, muses on what she can do about it, and confesses that she can't help herself.

The term "falling" is important when it comes to love and to life in general. When we fall, we have little control over ourselves and often hurt ourselves when we land. There is a kind of terror involved in falling, and that also applies to love and to finding a partner, someone to live with and perhaps someone to marry.

Dietrich points out that she's falling in love a*gain*, which suggests previous love affairs didn't work out to her satisfaction, but she is still committed to finding a love object. She muses about what to do and then confesses she can't help herself because "love is her game."

Choosing a partner (wife, husband, or someone to live with) is one of the most consequential actions people take since it is generally understood to be the beginning of a long-term relationship one is starting. If one makes the correct choice, the relationship lasts a lifetime. I write as someone married for 62 years.

There is a question about how people make their choices when it comes to marriage or any form of long-term relationship. Is it love and passion that is basic, or are there other factors involved in deciding to start a relationship? For example, a friend of mine married a Russian woman who used her sexuality to entice my friend but, once married, behaved in a way that he found unacceptable, leading to a quick divorce. But for her, she had American citizenship.

So, some relationships are not based on love but on other things. Some marriages are based on a desire to move up the socio-economic ladder and escape from poverty or from a middle-class status to that of wealth.

Aristotle pointed out that we are social animals in his *Politics*:

> Man is by nature a social animal; an individual who is unsocial naturally and not accidentally is either beneath our notice or more than human. Society is something that precedes the individual. Anyone who either cannot lead the common life or is so self-sufficient as not to need to, and therefore does not partake man-is by-nature-a-social-animal-an-individual is either a beast or a god.

Aristotle, *Politics*.

The basic institution for the socialization of children (and everyone else) is the family, of one kind or another, a dominant institution in all societies. It is forming families that is the ultimate (though not necessarily recognized) achievement of romantic love.

Melanie Klein, an English psychoanalyst, points out how love shapes our relationships with others and our thoughts about good and evil in ourselves. She writes in "Love, Greed and Aggression" in *Love, Hate and Reparation* (1964, 43-44):

> Now the man who has lost the woman he loves, or thinks he will lose her, is reacting not only to her love or his possession of her but also to the loss of them as proofs of his own value to himself, and so of his security in the world of his own mind, to say nothing of the outside world....A sexual partner—and to most people especially in the settled relation of marriage, where there is some responsibility on both sides—is felt to be a great recognition, and thus a proof, of that preponderance of good over evil in ourselves that we all seek, and on which our peace of mind depends....How much does this motive for the need for reassurance one's own value play a part in the decision of men and women to marry, and how little in comparison with it does the feeling of love or sexual desire impel them?

She suggests the need for reassurance is crucially important and may be more important than love or sexual desire, a view that many people, especially those not familiar with psychoanalytic theory, will find difficult to believe. But her argument that our need for love is our strongest protection against feelings of hate and destructiveness also lodged in our psyches, derived from our superegos and thus unrecognized, explains why love and marriage are so fragile.

Divorce in the USA

It is strange, if you think about it, how many people get divorced after a relatively short period of marriage. You have to wonder whether the burdens placed on marriage are too great since so many marriages end in divorce. Here is some information from a source about marriage:

> Marriage is an event that bonds two (or, rarely, more) people together for life, creating a legal, cultural, and/or religious connection between them that impacts everything from their name and address to their future family. Marriage is a cultural universal, an institution so fundamental to the human experience that there are no known examples of a society that functions without it. People marry for many reasons, including love, companionship, the desire to build a family, financial stability, social status, and religious fulfillment, and in nearly every case, the marriage

is considered a watershed event in the participants' lives. Sometimes, however, the bonds of marriage break. According to the United States' National Center for Health Statistics, approximately 4-5 million people get married every year in the U.S....and approximately 42-53% of those marriages eventually end in divorce.

World Population Review. (n.d.). "Divorce rates by country."

The following statistics from Divorce.com offer an insight into the prevalence and various aspects of divorce in the USA:

The United States has the sixth highest divorce rate in the world, with 40% to 50% of married couples filing for a divorce.

The United States Census Bureau report suggests that marriage and divorce rates dropped from 2009 to 2019.

Usually, second or third marriages in the United States have a higher divorce rate: 60% of second marriages and about 73% of third marriages end in divorce.

Couples going through their first divorce are around the age of 30. Married couples between the ages of 20 to 25 are 60% likely to get a divorce.

Black women divorce at a higher rate (38.9%) than women of any other race.

The military divorce rate is 3% on average. In 2019 alone, 30,608 military marriages ended in divorce.

Baby Boomers have the highest divorce rate among other generations, 34.9%.

Three states – Maryland, New Jersey, and Massachusetts – have some of the United States's highest median income levels and lowest rates of divorce.

Another Internet source I consulted pointed out that the average marriage that ends in divorce lasts eight years and that 86% of people who get divorced contemplate getting a divorce for a year before filing. In the USA, it costs around $15,000 for lawyer's fees, etc., to get divorced.

It is important to recognize that the states with the highest median incomes have the lowest rates of divorce, which suggests there is a correlation between income levels or socioeconomic status, which are affected by educational attainments and divorce.

Also, it may be the case that many people who marry have unrealistic expectations about what marriage is like and find that it doesn't provide the benefits and the gratifications they expected marriage would have.

Having a child also is a complication of marital relationships as wives become mothers, with different priorities than before they gave birth and different lifestyles and relationships between husbands and wives (or whoever is responsible for women becoming impregnated) after a child is born. Because of these factors, many women now have children without being married or even being in a stable relationship.

These divorce factors suggest that love, as traditionally defined, is now different and its relationship to our lives has changed in important ways.

An article in the February 21, 2023, *Marin Independent Journal titled "Single? You're Not Alone,"* suggests that many people now see a solo life as better for them. The article by Elizabeth Blake (originally published on the website, *The Conversation* reads (February 1, 2023, B1):

> Social practices that celebrate romance while ignoring the joys of friendship and solitude reflect widespread assumptions. One is that everyone is seeking a romantic relationship. The second is more value laden: Living in a long-term romantic, sexual partnership is better than living without one. This fuels belief that those living solo are less happy, or lonelier, than couples....The truth is that more Americans are living unmarried and without a romantic partner. In 2005, the census for the first time recorded a majority of women living outside marriage. By 2010, married couples became a minority in the United States....Changing family patterns are not simply the result of financial stability. They reflect choices. Not everyone wants a romantic partnership, and many single people see solo life as more conducive to flourishing and autonomy.

Blake points out that many women see married life as involving extra work for them and also that there are many people who can be described as asexual and aromantic. And many people living alone have many friendships.

So, it may be that the institution of marriage is too problematic for many people who, for one reason or another, choose to live alone. Alone, but not necessarily lonely or always by themselves.

The global COVID-19 pandemic blew up the traditional, in-the-office work week for a lot of people, but it didn't make achieving the elusive work-life balance easier, *Wall Street Journal* columnist Rachel Feintzeig told students at the Yale School of Management on February 13. "I think something has shifted, but I'm not sure where it's going to go," Feintzeig said. While remote work arrangements have made life less hectic for some workers, others feel isolated in at-home offices and anxious about missing out on valuable facetime with managers.

The problem isn't a new one. How to balance a successful career with a satisfying personal life "is one of the core never-ending questions of my column," said Feintzeig, the *Journal*'s "Work & Life" columnist. Feintzeig spoke at Yale SOM as part of the R. Peter Straus Lecture series. Named for R. Peter Straus YC '44, a pioneer in public-service radio, the series hosts talk with prominent individuals on topics related to the press and public responsibility. Yale SOM Dean Kerwin K. Charles moderated a discussion that touched on issues in today's evolving workplace, where a new generation is redefining success.

The quest for a healthier work and life mix is being driven by the growing ranks of remote-work and hybrid employees, as well as a new generation, who are realizing there are more important things in life than professional success, Feintzeig said. This realization has fueled the "quiet quitting" trend that's seen employees leaving the workforce or opting for reduced roles. At the same time, a new generation of workers, more invested in their personal lives, is seeking environments that foster work-life balance.

Karen Guzman. 2023, February 17. "Pursuing work-life balance in a post-pandemic world." *Yale School of Management.*

Chapter 8

Work

Most people spend a great deal of time working. People who work the traditional 9:00 AM to 5:00 PM spend a third of their day working, and some people often work overtime.

When we meet strangers at a party or wherever, it is not unusual for us to ask them, "what do you do?" We ask that question so we can get a sense of what they are like and can continue a conversation more easily. This question suggests that our occupations play a major role in our identities.

We can suggest two polarities which, while simplistic, provide an insight into how people think about work.

Table 8.1: Education and Work

College	High School
White-Collar Jobs	Blue-Collar Jobs
Affluent	Middle Class
Professional	Trades
Mind	Body
Create	Apply
Administrator	Worker

Table by the Author

This chart suggests the implications that stem from a difference in educational levels and provides us with an important insight into how to converse with people we meet.

But it doesn't work all the time. For example, my wife and I often use a handyman, who would seemingly fit under the High School category. But this handyman is a graduate of Amherst College, a very select institution, and also has a law degree. I assume he got burned out as a lawyer and enjoys being a handyman. And he is an excellent, I should add. Many years ago, we employed a plumber who had a Ph.D. in mathematics.

In the Bible, Adam and Eve in the Garden didn't work. They could remain in the Garden forever as long as they didn't eat an apple on the Tree of Knowledge. The snake persuaded Eve to eat an apple, and she persuaded Adam to do the same. When this happened, they realized they were naked, and God discovered they had eaten from the Tree of Knowledge and banished them from the Garden.

Now the serpent was more subtil than any beast of the field which the LORD God had made. And he said unto the woman, Yea, hath God said, Ye shall not eat of every tree of the garden? 2 And the woman said unto the serpent, We may eat of the fruit of the trees of the garden:3 But of the fruit of the tree which *is* in the midst of the garden, God hath said, Ye shall not eat of it, neither shall ye touch it, lest ye die. 4 And the serpent said unto the woman, Ye shall not surely die: 5 For God doth know that in the day ye eat thereof, then your eyes shall be opened, and ye shall be as gods, knowing good and evil. 6 And when the woman saw that the tree *was* good for food, and that it *was* pleasant to the eyes, and a tree to be desired to make *one* wise, she took of the fruit thereof, and did eat, and gave also unto her husband with her; and he did eat. 7 And the eyes of them both were opened, and they knew that they *were* naked; and they sewed fig leaves together, and made themselves aprons. 8 And they heard the voice of the LORD God walking in the garden in the cool of the day: and Adam and his wife hid themselves from the presence of the LORD God amongst the trees of the garden. 9 And the LORD God called unto Adam, and said unto him, Where *art* thou? 10 And he said, I heard thy voice in the garden, and I was afraid, because I *was* naked; and I hid myself. 11 And he said, Who told thee that thou *wast* naked? Hast thou eaten of the tree, whereof I commanded thee that thou shouldest not eat? 12 And the man said, The woman whom thou gavest *to be* with me, she gave me of the tree, and I did eat. 13 And the LORD God said unto the woman, What *is* this *that* thou hast done? And the woman said, The serpent beguiled me, and I did eat. 14 And the LORD God said unto the serpent, Because thou hast done this, thou *art* cursed above all cattle, and above every beast of the field; upon thy belly shalt thou go, and dust shalt thou eat all the days of thy life: 15 And I will put enmity between thee and the woman, and between thy seed and her seed; it shall bruise thy head, and thou shalt bruise his heel. 16 Unto the woman he said, I will greatly multiply thy sorrow and thy conception; in sorrow thou shalt bring forth children; and thy desire *shall be* to thy husband, and he shall rule over thee. 17 And unto Adam he said, Because thou hast hearkened unto the voice of thy wife, and hast eaten of the tree, of which I commanded thee, saying, Thou shalt not eat of it: cursed *is* the ground for thy sake; in sorrow shalt thou eat *of* it all the days of thy life; 18 Thorns also and thistles shall it bring forth to thee; and thou shalt eat the herb of the field; 19 In the sweat of thy face shalt thou eat bread, till thou return unto the ground; for out of it wast thou taken: for dust thou *art*, and unto dust shalt thou return.

King James Bible Online. (n.d.). *Genesis 3:1-19.*

The important line here, in terms of work, is "In the sweat of thy face shalt thou eat bread till thou return to the ground; for out of it wast thou taken: for dust though *art* and into dust shall thou return."

The story of Adam and Eve in the Garden of Eden is one of the foundational myths in the Western world and the fact that man had to work has shaped much of the thinking and the development of social, cultural, and economic institutions in many countries, leading eventually to the development of capitalism.

Several scholars, such as Max Weber, have written about the development of the capitalist socio-economic order. Weber linked it to Protestantism. But it was Karl Marx who offered the most systematic discussion of the rise of capitalism and the role that elites, members of the ruling classes, play in capitalist societies.

Marx wrote about the development of capitalism, an economic system in which "the ruling class" shapes the thinking and behavior of the masses, the working class or "proletariat" and exploits them with terrible consequences.

One of the worst consequences of capitalism, he explained, involves the alienation of workers from themselves and from others (1964, 169-170):

> In what does this alienation of labour consist? First, that the work is *external* to the worker, that it is not a part of his nature, that consequently he does not fulfill himself in his work but denies himself, has a feeling of misery, not of wellbeing, does not develop freely a physical and mental energy, but is physically exhausted and mentally debased. The worker therefore feels himself at home only during his leisure, whereas at work he feels homeless. His work is not voluntary but imposed, *forced labour.* It is not the satisfaction of a need, but only a *means* for satisfying other needs. Its alien character is clearly shown by the fact that as soon as there is no physical or other compulsion, it is avoided like the plague. Finally, the alienated character of work for the worker appears in the fact that it is not his work but work for someone else, that in work he does not belong to himself but to another person....
>
> The *alienation* of the worker in his product means not only that his labour becomes an object, takes on its own existence, but that it exists outside him, independently, and alien to him, and that it stands opposed to him as an autonomous power. The life which he has given to the object sets itself against him as an alien and hostile force.

This alienation leads to people becoming separated or estranged from their work, from their friends, and from themselves. When people's work, which is central to their identity and sense of self, becomes separated from themselves or their "selves," work ends up as a destructive force.

This leads to workers experiencing themselves as objects, things that are acted upon, and not as subjects, active forces in the world. The things people produce become "commodities," objects separated, somehow, from their labor. As people become increasingly more alienated, they become the prisoners of their alienated needs and end up, as Marx puts it, "the *self-conscious* and *self-acting* commodity." (Quoted in Erich Fromm, 1962, 51).

An article by Roberta Rosa Valtorta and Maria Grazia Monaci, (in the *European Journal of Psychology*), "When Workers Feel Like Objects: A Field Study on Self-Objectification and Affective Organizational Commitment," discusses this matter of objectification in some detail:

> The philosopher Martha Nussbaum (1995) specified seven ways to objectify a person, including treating others as instrumental, fungible, violable and owned as well as denying others autonomy, agency, and subjectivity. During the last decades, social psychology has generally focused on sexual objectification, that is, the experience of being treated as a body (or collection of body parts) valued predominantly for its use to (or consumption by) others....However, objectification is a much broader phenomenon that may encompass many human interactions and domains. Perceiving others as mere objects is indeed a powerful cognitive strategy that rationalizes their exploitation or subordination (Volpato et al., 2017). Marx (1844) claimed that workers in a capitalistic society are denied the traits that define their humanity and are judged exclusively for what they produce. In Marx's view, the capitalist model's goal is to produce wealth, and workers are the essential instruments in creating this wealth. Although these reflections may appear to belong to a past era, workers' objectification still permeates many workplaces. A report (BBC, 2013) documented the object-like treatment of Amazon "order-pickers." Their daily activity is highly repetitive, imposed by a timer, and mostly limited to picking orders from supervisors and finding products in the warehouse. More recently, a former worker at Amazon's Swansea warehouse has claimed that clerks were treated like robots and routinely sacked for not meeting "unrealistic targets" (BBC, 2018). Similarly, a picker at a warehouse in Minnesota has stated that Amazon workers were considered more similar to machines than human beings (BBC, 2019).

There is a debate among Marxist scholars about whether to see alienation or the need for revolution as basic to Marxist thinking. Whatever the case, his comments about alienation suggest there is a humanist element in his thinking. Marxists argue that capitalism dealt with the danger of revolution by creating consumer cultures, which distracted people from recognizing their exploitation and helped assuage their feelings of alienation.

The most important event involving work in recent times was the COVID-19 pandemic. It disrupted work arrangements everywhere and has led to new perspectives on work for many people. They found they liked not having to go to the office every day, avoiding the need to commute, and could do their work at home in a more pleasant (and less dangerous) atmosphere.

My daughter, a psychoanalyst, gave up her office and now conducts all her therapeutic sessions on Zoom. She says her patients also prefer that arrangement since they don't have to commute to her office and worry about parking, among other things. My son, who works for Google, only goes into the office to work two days a week now, though we don't know how long Google will allow workers to work from their homes.

The price people who work from home pay is a lack of social relationships and a sense of isolation, but maybe coming to the office two or three days a week solves those problems.

In the United States, people started looking at work in a new way. American workers don't have holidays that are as long as European workers. In turn, many Americans are both changing the way they work and how they think about work.

A recent *Washington Post* article on four-day workweeks offers some insights into the changes that may come to the traditional workweek.

Dozens of companies there took part in the world's largest trial of the four-day workweek — and a majority of supervisors and employees liked it so much they've kept the arrangement. In fact, 15 percent of the employees who participated said "no amount of money" would convince them to go back to working five days a week.

Nearly 3,000 employees took part in the pilot, which was organized by the advocacy group 4 Day Week Global, in collaboration with the research group Autonomy, and researchers at Boston College and the University of Cambridge.

Companies that participated could adopt different methods to "meaningfully" shorten their employees' workweeks — from giving them one day a week off to reducing their working days in a year to average out to 32 hours per week — but had to ensure the employees still received 100 percent of their pay.

Annabelle Timsit. 2023, February 21. "Four-day workweek gains momentum in the UK." *The Washington Post.*

Because of COVID-19, there have been many important changes in the lifestyles of people everywhere, and it is reasonable to assume that something like the four-day workweek will spread to many countries.

For many workers, the COVID-19 pandemic led to a radical change in their attitudes toward work, and something like three million workers disappeared from the workplace in what has been called the "great resignation." Some of these workers retired early, and some just left the workforce. Whatever the case, people's attitudes towards work and where one works have changed in remarkable ways.

For decades, owning a home has been seen as a hallmark of the "American dream" and a major life milestone. It's "embedded in how we think about real estate," Mark Eppli, director of the James A. Graaskamp Center for Real Estate at the University of Wisconsin-Madison, tells CNBC Make It. And purchasing a home is a way to build generational wealth.

Things may be changing, however. For many millennials, home ownership is out of reach. About one in three millennials under the age of 35 owned a home at the end of 2018, according to the U.S. Census Bureau. That number is eight to nine percentage points lower than Baby Boomers and Gen X homeownership rates at ages 25 to 34.

But what does that mean for the happiness of those who can't or won't buy a home? Is buying a home really a key to happiness, or just another source of stress?

As humans, we have an evolutionary need for stability, community, and neighborhood, which owning a home can provide, Christine Carter, a sociologist and senior fellow at the Greater Good Science Center at the University of California Berkeley, tells CNBC Make It.

Research suggests that, as far as happiness is concerned, owning a home is no better than renting.

Cory Stieg. 2020, October 27. "Does buying a home make you happier? The psychology of home ownership." *CNBC.*

Chapter 9

Housing

After I got my Ph.D. from the University of Minnesota in 1965, I got a job at San Francisco State University, and my wife and I and our daughter lived in an apartment in San Francisco. We had a son while living in the city and stayed there until our children needed to go to school.

That led to a period of looking around for a house to live in, which took several months before we found one in a small town, Mill Valley, located about eight miles north of the Golden Gate Bridge in Marin County.

We bought our house in 1970 and are still in the same house. We also liked the fact that it had enough rooms so my wife and I could have separate studies.

Figure 9.1: Our Living Room

But finding that house was an ordeal for us, to put it mildly, and it turned out that we looked at over forty houses before we made a decision. And that is typical for many people who move to cities without good school districts. Eventually, many city dwellers with children move to other cities or to suburbs with excellent school districts so their children will get a good education.

Figure 9.2: Dining Room

Buying a house is the biggest investment most people make and generally involves looking at many houses before choosing one. There are a variety of reasons why people buy a particular house.

Sometimes, it is the cost of the house that is critical. In other cases, people want to live near friends or "fall in love" with the design of the house. In our case, we found a house near the schools that our children would attend, whose design we liked (we could have a table in the kitchen, a dining room, and a back deck, and it had enough rooms so our children each could have their own room). And we had a spectacular view. We also liked the spatiality of the top floor of our house with its high ceilings. Our house is basically a library with bedrooms. I built fourteen large bookcases, and we have thousands of books.

People who are wealthy tend to buy homes in upscale neighborhoods with other large and fancy homes because of their desire to live with people of the same socioeconomic status. Birds of a feather flock together. In recent years, we've discovered that many people search for areas to buy their homes where people have the same politics.

Owning a home is part of the American Dream, but it turns out that many people who purchase homes don't recognize the negative aspects of home ownership, such as the cost of repairs needed to keep up a home.

In our case, over the years, we had to replace the back deck, which was falling apart, and the kitchen, which was not in good shape, and we also changed all the windows, which were single-paned, and had to install a new water heater and purchase new stoves, refrigerators and dishwashers. When you live in a house for fifty years, you must devote a certain amount of money to upkeep. On the other hand, purchasing a home is a major investment that generally increases in value and is a source of wealth for many homeowners. In Mill Valley, in my neighborhood, houses that cost $40,000 in 1970 are now worth more than a million dollars and some two million dollars. People like me, who bought our homes many years ago, are "grandfathered in" and own homes we could never afford if we wanted to buy one now, in our neighborhood.

Many people who purchase homes make major changes in them.

One of my neighbors, who purchased a home that friends of ours lived in, completely restructured the house. He purchased the house for two million dollars and must have spent another million dollars changing it all around. My wife and I were out on a walk when a car pulled over and the driver started chatting with us. He then invited us to see his house, so when we finished our walk, we went to see his house.

It was a spectacular transformation. Remarkably, the house was originally very nice when he purchased it, but he had his own ideas about what it should look like and retained a very talented architect to change everything. It is not unusual for people to change their kitchens when they purchase a house. I have several friends who installed a new kitchen as a selling point in houses they were selling, who tell me that the new owner immediately got rid of the new kitchen and installed another one.

Many people don't make major changes in their homes since it is so expensive, and, for many people, owning a home is a financial burden, especially since homes have become so expensive. People's choices in homes, many times, are based on what they can afford and thus are limited, though nowadays, many people spend more on a home than they can afford and devote a major percentage of their income to housing. There is such a demand for housing in the San Francisco Bay Area that people often bid more than a house is listed for by real estate agents.

It is the high cost of housing that helps explain why so many people are homeless or "unhoused" as we describe the phenomenon now. We have not built enough homes for the population in California, and increasing numbers of people now find themselves homeless, a genuine tragedy for them and American society.

U.S. TOURISM STATISTICS:

- **US Citizen domestic tourism:** Americans take 2.29 Billion domestic trips each year.

- **US Citizen outbound tourism:** Americans take 93.0 Million international outbound trips each year.

- **International Inbound Tourism:** Annually, there are currently 79.6 million international visitors to the U.S.

- **$1,089 Billion:** Yearly American tourism expenditure ($932.7b domestic / $156.3b international)

- **Expenditure sources:** $267.7B on food services, $232.2B on lodging, $200.4B on public transport, $166.5B on auto transportation, $112.6B on recreation, $109.6B on retail.

- **15.7 Million** American jobs were supported by travel in 2018.

- **By 2028,** yearly U.S. tourism is estimated to hit the $2.4 trillion mark.

- Days/yr. traveled by age group: Gen Z **(29 days)**, Millennials **(35 days)**, Gen X **(26 days)** and Baby Boomers **(27 days).**

- **Top 5 inbound countries:** Mexico (19.1m), Canada (12.3m), UK (4.9), Japan (3.4), China (2.9)

- **Top 5 outbound by continent:** Europe (17.7m), Caribbean (8.7m), Asia (6.2m), South America (2.1m), Central America (3.2m)

- **Top U.S. cities visited:** New York (9.8m), Miami (5.38m), LA (4.98m), Orlando (4.47m), San Francisco (3.57m), Vegas (3.33m)

- **Business vs. leisure:** U.S. travelers took 466.2 million domestic trips for business (26.2%), and 1,779.7 million for leisure (73.8%)

Tourism Academy. 2021, September 15. "U.S. Tourism Travel Statistics 2020-2021."

Chapter 10

Ocean Cruising Tourism

Tourism is one of the largest industries in the world. Before COVID-19, every year, more than one billion people traveled to foreign destinations, and countless billions traveled within the borders of their countries.

The statistics on tourism in America offer a snapshot of the size and scope of the tourism industry and its impact on the American economy, on American society, and on American culture as a whole.

Let me begin by trying to answer a complicated question: what is a tourist? For my answer, I offer this definition from Dean MacCannell's influential book, *The Tourist: A New Theory of the Leisure Class* (1976, 1):

> "TOURIST" is used to mean two things. It designates actual tourists: sightseers, mainly middle class, who are at the moment deployed throughout the entire world in search of experience…. The tourist is an actual person, or real people are actually tourists. At the same time, "the tourist is one of the best models available for modern-man-in-general."

That is a broad but useful definition. MacCannell is interested in tourists because he sees them (1976, 1) as "one of the best models available for modern-man-in general….Our first apprehension of modern civilization, it seems to me, emerges in the mind of the tourist."

The United Nations World Tourism Organization defines tourism in a more direct manner:

> It comprises the actions of persons traveling to and staying in places outside their usual environment for not more than one consecutive year for leisure, business, and other purposes not related to the exercise of an activity remunerated from within the place visited.

Between the MacCannell and World Tourism Organization definitions, we have a pretty good idea of what tourists are and what tourism involves.

An Israeli sociologist, Erik Cohen, suggests there are four kinds of tourists in his article, "Toward a Sociology of International Tourism" (in Charles R. Goeldner, et al. *Tourism: Principles, Practices, Philosophies*. Eighth Edition. New York: John Wiley & Sons. 1990, 341):

Institutionalized

Individual mass: These are tourists who go to an agency in search of tourist information. They make individual trips, taking advantage of the destination's infrastructure established for mass tourism.

Organized mass: These travelers take organized tours where all the details are covered, and there are no surprises of any kind. It is usually family tourism without any major variations.

Non-institutionalized

Drifter: This is the independent tourist who backpacks. They do not depend on the infrastructure and have little influence on the destination, as they interact with the environment and usually integrate with it.

Explorer: This is the tourist who seeks new experiences, often extreme. The definition they use is "off the beaten track." They prioritize the experience and can sacrifice comforts.

Perhaps the most famous tourism typology was made by Stanley Plog and appeared in his article, "Why Destinations Arise and Fail in Popularity," which appeared in the *Cornell University Hotel and Restaurant Administration Quarterly* (Vol. 43, No.2, June 2001). It argues that there are five kinds of tourists based on their psychological state and tolerance of anxiety:

Allocentric

Near Allocentric

Mid-Centric

Near Psychocentric

Psychocentric

Plog's typology is a segmentation model that divides tourists into three groups based on their psychographic characteristics and travel behaviors. The three groups are:

1. Psychocentrics: These tourists prefer familiar destinations and are risk averse. They tend to travel in large groups, choose package tours, and prefer destinations with established infrastructure and amenities.

2. Mid-Centrics: These tourists fall between psychocentrics and allocentrics in terms of their psychographic profile. They are somewhat adventurous but still seek some degree of familiarity and comfort in their travel experiences.

3. Allocentrics: These tourists are the most adventurous and seek out new and exotic destinations. They are risk-takers and enjoy independent travel, seeking out unique experiences off the beaten path.

Plog's typology has been widely used in the tourism industry to segment markets and develop marketing strategies tailored to the needs and preferences of different types of travelers. However, some critics argue that the model oversimplifies the complex motivations and behaviors of tourists and that it is becoming outdated in an era of increasingly diverse and complex travel patterns.

There are many other typologies involving tourism that scholars have developed, just as there are many kinds of tourism one can choose from, such as religious tourism, cultural tourism, food tourism, sports tourism, events tourism, sex tourism, disaster tourism, and medical tourism.

Ocean Cruising

One of the most interesting developments in the tourism industry is the growth of ocean cruising. An internet search offers the following statistics:

The cruise industry made **$18B in revenue** in 2022. The total number of cruise ship passengers stood at 13M+ as of 2021. The cruise industry is expected to reach $25.1B in revenue by the end of 2023. The cruise industry supports over 1M jobs. A cruise costs an average of $214 per passenger daily. The world's fleet of cruise ships totals 430.

Adam Grucela. 2023, June 12. "Cruise industry statistics." *Passport Photo Online.*

As one might expect, there are different categories of cruise lines, from super-luxury lines, such as Regent Seven Seas, to relatively inexpensive lines, such as Carnival.

Fodors, a travel guide publisher, suggests there are only three main categories of ocean cruise ships: mainstream, premium and luxury. This typology is, to my mind, a bit too broad. There are other typologies of cruise lines that offer us an insight into the wide variety of possibilities available for ocean cruise takers.

Allthingscruise.com offers a more comprehensive typology of kinds of cruise lines. Below are the categories and some ships in the category

Contemporary
Aida
Carnival
Costa

Upscale Contemporary
MSC
Norwegian
Royal Caribbean

Premium
Celebrity
Disney
Holland America
Princess

Ultra Premium
Cunard
Oceania
Viking
Windstar

Ultra Luxury
Paul Gauguin
Regent Seven Seas
Seabourn
Seven Seas

Cruise Line Types. (n. d). *All Things Cruise.*

There are, I might add, other typologies with slightly different names for the categories, but this list of kinds of cruise lines offers a useful overview of the choices one can make when booking a cruise.

During my travels, my wife and I have been on MSC, Norwegian, Holland America, Royal Caribbean, and Princess, as well as other lines no longer in business, and can say that the lines are all distinctive and sailing on different ships in the same line can be a considerably different cruise experience.

My wife and I took our first cruise from San Francisco to Alaska, many years ago. I found the experience both pleasant and extremely interesting.

I took notes in my journal about the cruise and topics I wanted to write about, and when we returned home, I wrote articles about the semiotics of cruising, offered a psychoanalytic interpretation of cruising, wrote about cruising from a Marxist and from a sociological perspective, and then thought about finding scholarly journals in which to publish the articles.

I did not know that there were so many scholarly journals devoted to tourism and sent off queries to journals that I thought might find one of my articles worth publishing. A few days later, I got a reply from a professor, Kaye Chon, at Hong Kong Polytechnic University, who asked, "Is this a book?" I replied,

"It can be, if I add a few things to it," and he answered, saying he would like to see the manuscript when it was finished.

I added some data that those interested in tourism might find interesting and sent him the manuscript. He replied that he liked it and thus, *Ocean Tourism and Cruising* was published in 2004 by Haworth, a publisher of tourism books, and became the first of half a dozen books I was to write on some aspect of tourism.

At the time, I didn't realize how many universities offered courses and degrees on tourism at the bachelor's, master's and doctoral levels.

Figure 10.1: Ocean Travel and Cruising

Kaye Chon was, it turned out, the director of the Hong Kong Polytechnic School of Journalism and an influential figure in tourism scholarship. He later suggested I write about tourism in Asia-Pacific countries, which led me to write books such as *Vietnam Tourism, Thailand Tourism,* and *Tourism in Japan.* These are not travel books, but books about the cultures in these countries, though the books do deal with important tourist sites.

A friend of mine, who is a high-end luxury travel agent, offers an insight into the luxury cruise category. I asked her some questions about luxury cruising, and she provided the following answers:

1. **What are the most important luxury cruise lines?**
   Seabourn, Crystal, Silverseas, Abercrombie and Kent small ship cruising, Tauck small ship cruising. **On what basis do your customers choose their cruise lines? Is it certain ships? Itineraries? Something else?**

   Mostly, they choose from the cruise line with which they are familiar; secondly, by the itinerary.

2. **Do your customers tend to choose certain cruise lines? If so, why?**
    Loyalty to a certain cruise line is often the reason, as returning passengers or guests receive valuable amenities such as shipboard credit, free WIFI, advanced dining and shore excursion reservations, discounts for onboard purchases, spa discounts, etc.

4. **Have there been any interesting changes in the luxury cruise line business? Are there any changes relating to luxury tourism in general?**
    Yes, changes! "Expedition-designed luxury ships" are IN, to travel to the polar regions and more remote destinations. More educational onboard offerings such as photo workshops, cooking classes, lectures related to destinations, tech workshops, and experiential shore excursions that go beyond bus-touring.

5. **What thoughts do you have about the luxury cruise business and how it relates to luxury tourism, in general.**
    As the luxury traveler ages, cruising is becoming more desirable due to less packing/unpacking, ease of meals, and seamless service from airport to ship; all-inclusive pricing is also very appealing to many travelers, irrespective of age.

    Since COVID, some services and the quality and quantity of experienced personnel have challenged the tourism industry. Some guests have had to "lower their expectations" as the travel world is ever-evolving. **Pack patience and kindness** is a good motto! Another motto to live by: **Everything's fine until it's not!** (Flight delays, missed connections, poor in-flight service and food, unpredictable weather, unpredictable service, high prices, etc.)

We must remember that it is not unusual for luxury cruise lines to charge a minimum of one thousand dollars a night per passenger for their cruises. For example, Regent Seven Seas Cruises advertises a ten-night cruise from Barcelona to Venice, departing April 19, 2023, at the following prices:

Distinctive Suites:	From $17,499 per person
Penthouse Suites	From $13,749 per person
Concierge Suites	From $12,899 per person
Deluxe Veranda Suites	From $11,799 per person

These prices include free Business Class Air, but as you can see, it is very expensive to take a cruise on Seven Seas and other luxury lines.

Bob Dickinson and Andy Vladimir's *Selling the Seas: An Inside Look at the Cruise Industry* offers some information about the role of food in luxury cruise lines (1997, 47):

Marine architects now work with chefs and marketing executives to determine what the target market for a new ship will be and thus the menu is specifically designed to please that market. Only once the food is selected are the galley size and the equipment needed determined—not before.

For instance, when Seabourn commissioned its two ships, its research showed that upscale travelers regarded the perceived quality of a line's cuisine as the single most important factor in the success or failure of the entire cruise. They recognized that all meals on this luxurious vessel would need to be true haute cuisine—or as they called it, "Nouvelle Classic." This style of food would be cooked to order—a la minute—and there would be special orders that were not on the menu. Two more considerations at this point in the planning process were the amount of space that had been set aside for the galley and the number of crew available.

In essence, luxury cruise liners are designed to provide their passengers with the highest quality of food, cooked to order for each passenger, unlike resort-style food, cooked for large numbers of people, that one gets on less expensive lines. I should point out that cruise ships in all categories have increased the quality of the food they serve, and my wife and I have had many exceptional meals on our cruises.

At the other end of the spectrum, there is a ten-day Princess cruise from San Francisco to Mexico and back for less than the price of one day on a Regent Seven Seas voyage. The price for this cruise, in an inside cabin (which some cruise takers prefer), is $698. To this, you must add tips and other charges, but you can see that sailing on Princess can be relatively inexpensive.

Here is a report from a friend of mine, a former college professor, on his cruise on a Princess ship that left from Texas and visited ports in the Caribbean:

1. **What made you decide to take an ocean cruise?**
   Desire to get away to some place warm during the slow Christmas to New Year week and reports from like-minded friends that they had enjoyed cruises.

2. **What factors made you decide to choose the line you did?**
   Reasonable pricing plus trips during my time frame to close and warm places.

3. **How would you describe your experiences on the cruise?**
   Life on board was lovely, but on-shore experiences were awful.

4. **Did having an inside cabin cause any problems?**
   No. The inside cabin was quiet and beautiful.

5. **What do you have to say about the passengers on the ship?**
    Mostly from rural and suburban Texas because Galveston was the
    embarkation point. They were all very pleasant, but we had nothing in
    common ideologically or socially. This applies only to the folks with
    whom I dined. Almost all cruise from one to 9 months a year and don't
    have any other major interests.

6. **How would you describe the food on the ship? The service?**
    The food was gorgeous and elegant, with great variety. Maybe a bit
    under seasoned. The service was astounding. So courteous, helpful
    and attentive.

7. **Do you plan to take another cruise, or was that one enough?**
    If my health declined so I could not take a more active or strenuous
    trip, I would go again. I would embark from a location where more
    compatible folks would board and would hope to meet some Europeans,
    etc. I would barely consider the itinerary since the stops are in dumps
    or shopping centers, or if in interesting spots, then it is too brief.

8. **Any general comments of interest about your cruise or cruising, in
    general, would be appreciated...relative to other traveling you have
    done over the years.**
    Only to repeat: the on-board experiences of the shows, food, and
    fitness center were wonderful. The people were not interesting. The
    shore experiences were a total waste of time. I would only go again if
    my health didn't allow for something more active.

We must keep in mind that my friend, who has a Ph.D. in philosophy and
worked for many years as a CPA, is not your typical American.

Over the course of the years, the industry has changed considerably and now
some less expensive lines, such as Royal Caribbean and Norwegian, have
introduced remarkable innovations in cruise design, which makes choosing
cruises by category less meaningful. It is now not only the line, but particular
ships in that line, which is important.

Cruising is interesting from a psychoanalytic perspective. One thing that
attracted my attention was the number of cruises some ocean cruising fans
have taken. I've met people who have taken sixty, seventy, and eighty cruises—
some of which are quite long: thirty to sixty days.

Ocean cruising must satisfy some important gratifications that repeat
(obsessive?) cruisers desire. Cruising can be a powerful and expensive addiction. I
can recall meeting one couple on a cruise who told me they had booked four
cruises for the next year, one for 32 weeks, starting shortly after the cruise we
were on, docked.

Cruising may be a regressive experience, and cruise takers enjoy being in a situation where there is a return to their early years when they experienced unconditional "love" or, on the cruise, having their every need taken care of by the always obliging crew staff.

There are some negatives to ocean cruising. Some people find them boring. Even inexpensive cruises can become expensive if one takes excursions, drinks a lot, and gambles. And some people, such as my friend quoted above, find their fellow passengers not to their liking.

Since there are so many cruise lines and ships, choosing which line to sail on becomes increasingly difficult. The lines provide incentives for people to continue to cruise with them. Thus, for example, my wife and I have taken six cruises on Princess and now get free Internet. The more cruises you take on a line, the more incentives they offer, so it is easy to get "hooked" and continue to sail on a certain line.

Taking ocean cruises has become very popular, and many cruise lines report they are fully booked as cruise lovers seek to make up for the cruises they missed due to COVID-19, in what has been described as an example of "revenge cruising."

My wife and I, after being cooped up in our house for almost four years, are typical revenge tourists and have booked three cruises over the next two years to make up for what we missed when confined to our home. I am immunocompromised and only recently did my oncologist tell me it would not be too risky for me to take a cruise. Once he told me I could return to cruising, we booked the cruises—all from San Francisco, so we don't have to fly anywhere.

Lesbian, gay, bisexual, transgender

LGBTQIA+ is an abbreviation for **lesbian, gay, bisexual, transgender**, queer or questioning, intersex, asexual, and more. These terms are used to describe a person's sexual orientation or gender identity.

Gender dysphoria is a term that describes a sense of unease that a person may have because of a mismatch between their biological sex and their gender identity. This sense of unease or dissatisfaction may be so intense it can lead to depression and anxiety and have a harmful impact on daily life.

Gender identity refers to our sense of who we are and how we see and describe ourselves. Most people identify as "male" or "female". These are sometimes called "binary" identities. However, some people feel their gender identity is different from their biological sex. For example, some people may have male genitals and facial hair but do not identify as male or feel masculine. Some may have female genitals and breasts but do not identify as female or feel feminine. Some people do not define themselves as having a "binary" identity. For them, the concept of gender is not relevant to their identity.

They may use different terms, such as gender, gender diverse, or gender non-conforming, to describe their identity. However, as a group, they are often called "non-binary." Many people with gender dysphoria have a strong, lasting desire to live a life that "matches" or expresses their gender identity. They do this by changing the way they look and behave. Some people with gender dysphoria, but not all, may want to use hormones and sometimes surgery to express their gender identity. Gender dysphoria is not a mental illness, but some people may develop mental health problems because of gender.

NHS. (n.d.). "Gender dysphoria."

Chapter 11

Gender Choice

For many people, the idea that people can choose their gender is absurd. In the Bible, we learned that God created man and then, so he would not be alone, created woman and the notion that a woman could change her gender and become a man, or a man could change his gender and become a woman is simply preposterous. Gender, they believe, is binary and based on the natural opposition of man and woman.

And yet, we now have a movement in which gender is now seen as fluid and non-binary and a choice that people can make. The LGBTQIA+ movement stands for:

Lesbian
Gay
Bisexual
Transgender
Queer (or questioning)
Intersexual
Asexual
And more

The Gallup Poll offers us some statistics on the subject:

WASHINGTON, D.C. – After showing perceptible increases in 2020 and 2021, U.S. adults' identification as lesbian, gay, bisexual, transgender or something other than heterosexual held steady in 2022, at 7.2%. The current percentage is double what it was when Gallup first measured LGBT identification a decade ago.

The data are based on aggregated polling data from 2022 Gallup telephone surveys, encompassing interviews with over 10,000 U.S. adults. In each survey, Gallup asks respondents if they identify as lesbian, gay, bisexual, transgender or something else, allowing them to choose multiple identities.

In addition to the 7% identifying as LGBT, 86% of U.S. adults say they are straight or heterosexual, while 7% chose not to answer the question.
As is typically the case, the greatest share of LBGT adults–more than half, or 4.2% of all U.S. adults– identify as bisexual. About one in five LGBT adults identify as gay, about one in seven say they are lesbian, and slightly fewer than one in 10 identify as transgender.

Five percent of LGBT adults identify as something other than lesbian, gay, bisexual or transgender. In 2022, Gallup for the first time recorded the preferred identity of those who indicated they were something other than heterosexual besides the traditional lesbian, gay, bisexual or transgender identities. Most of these individuals said they were queer, pansexual or asexual. Roughly 1%-2% of LGBT adults--equivalent to 0.1% of all U.S. adults -- prefer each of those identities.

Jeffrey M. Jones. 2023, February 22. "U.S. LGBT Identification Steady at 7.2%." *Gallup.*

This means that around 20 million people identify as LGBTQIA+, while 86% of Americans identify themselves as "straight" (or heterosexual), and the rest don't choose to identify themselves at all.

Until relatively recently, men who were homosexuals, as they were commonly described, and women who were lesbians, kept their sexual preferences hidden and lived, so to speak, in the shadows. There have been many prominent artists and writers who were homosexuals or lesbians throughout history, such as Leonardo da Vinci, Caravaggio, John Cage, Elizabeth Bishop and Djuna Barnes (and countless others).

Now, in America, we find that many gay men and lesbian women (and those with other gender identities) marry and raise children, and that many politicians are now "openly gay," as they are commonly described by the press.

Figure 11.1: Judith Butler

Judith Butler, a professor at the University of California at Berkeley, is a leading theorist of gender. Gender, she argues in her influential book, *Gender Trouble*, is best seen as a performance and is socially constructed. It is not a binary matter of being either male or female. So, gender, we may say, is based on choices people make and not solely on biology.

In the first chapter of *Gender Trouble*, titled "Subjects of Sex/Gender/Desire," Butler discusses the relationship that exists between sex and gender (1999, 9,10):

Originally intended to dispute the biology-is-destiny formulation, the distinction between sex and gender serves the argument that whatever biological intractability sex appears to have, gender is culturally constructed: hence, gender is neither the casual result of sex nor as seemingly fixed as sex....If gender is the cultural meanings that the sexed body assumes, then gender cannot be said to follow from a sex in any one way. Taken to its logical limit, the sex/gender distinction suggests a radical discontinuity between sexed bodies and culturally constructed genders. Assuming for the moment the stability of binary sex, it does not follow that the construction of "men" will accrue exclusively to the bodies of males or that "women" will interpret only female bodies. Further, even if the sexes appear to be unproblematically binary in their morphology and constitution (which will become a question), there is no reason to assume that genders ought also to remain at two.

Here, Butler argues, gender is not "fixed" at birth but is socially constructed. This suggests that one can change one's gender since it does not automatically follow from one's sex "in any way." Her book is an attempt to disrupt the conventional ways that people think about gender and sexuality. The LGBTIQ+ movement is a testimonial to that matter.

Semioticians explain that binary thinking is basic to the way the mind works. In his book *Semiotics: The Basics*, third edition, Daniel Chandler writes (2017, 107):

As Jonathan Culler notes, "The advantage of binarism, but also its principal danger, lies in the fact that it permits one to classify anything" (1975, 15). Binarism is rightly criticized when it leads to negative stereotyping and when it is uncritically accepted as "the real"—as in commonsense assumptions that supposedly either/or oppositions such as male and female, or heterosexual and homosexual exhaust the possibilities of the domains they purport to encompass....Our entire system of values is built upon oppositions, which exist within sign systems rather than in the world.

He quotes sociologist Eviatar Zerubavel, who writes (2017, 107):

Our entire social order is a product of the ways in which we separate kin from non-kin, moral from immoral, serious from merely playful, and what is ours from what is not.

Chandler adds (2017, 107), "We live within a world constructed from such oppositions, so they have very real consequences." His point is that our thinking is largely based upon oppositions, but these oppositions often are simplistic. I would suggest that in the popular mind, something like the following binary oppositions exist relative to gender:

Table 11.1: Male-Female Binary Oppositions

Male	Female
Cisgender	Transgender
Normal	Abnormal
Rigid	Flexible
Straight	Gay
Binary	Non-Binary

Table by the Author

There are certain elements of non-binary lives that are of some consequence, such as the problem of sexually transmitted infections. Sexually transmitted infections have been growing rapidly, according to an article, "Antibiotics After Sex Cuts Risk of Infections for Some, Studies Show," by Apoorva Mandavilli, in the March 10, 2022, issue of the *New York Times* (page A16).

Certain members of the LGBTQIA+ community are affected by the growth of these diseases. She writes:

> The strategy has been shown to work among trans women and men who have sex with men who are at high risk for acquiring an S.T.I. But the pills have not shown a benefit in cisgender women (whose gender identity matches the sex assigned at birth).

We can infer from this article that sex and gender can have a complicated and, in some cases, problematic relationship.

One of the most important aspects of the LGBTQIA+ movement is that binary distinctions are inadequate and misleading. Gender is a very complex subject, and we can see from statistics on gender that were quoted earlier in this chapter that many millions of people do not accept the binary perspective on gender and are leading normal lives, in many respects, such as marrying, raising children, and becoming politicians--lives that could now be described as mainstream, most Americans would say.

On the other hand, there are many political attacks on the LGBT community in conservative Republican states, as a report on ABC explains:

> Republicans have introduced more than 300 anti-LGBTQ bills and at least nine states have signed at least one into law. Some conservatives say they are fighting for parents to have more of a say over what their children learn in school and have passed laws restricting LGBTQ content in some classrooms. Others say children should not be allowed to transition even with parental permission and have banned hormone therapies or implemented policies against social transitioning for trans

youth. Equality Texas CEO Ricardo Martinez says anti-LGBTQ legislation and rhetoric "empowers folks who have an animus against us to use us as targets." Martinez says his local LGBTQ advocacy group has seen a marked increase in the number of reports of trans people being bullied or attacked. Anti-transgender hate crimes in particular have continued to climb year after year, according to FBI data.

Kiara Alfonseca. 2022, June 21. "Threats and violence: LGBTQ community faces renewed political battles during Pride Month." *ABC News.*

Though most Americans accept the LGBTQ community, many do not, and gender remains an unresolved problem for American society and politics.

The big push of interest in the subject of creativity began in 1950 when J. P. Guilford of the University of Southern California was president of the American Psychological Association. Guilford said in his presidential address to that organization that he found an appalling lack of research on creativity. He said he had searched Psychological Abstracts for a quarter of a century and found that only 186 out of 121,000 entries dealt in any way with creativity, imagination, or any topic closely related. In the years since 1950, more than a dozen books have appeared on the subject, and I have approximately 300 reference cards to articles and monographs. The research undertaken since Guilford gave his speech has yielded results of basic significance to the field of education and to the archives of knowledge. These studies have rendered into baloney many former sacred cows. For instance, the idea that the IQ is a lump sum and that it is constant, the idea that "well-adjusted children" (often meaning conformers) will become the most useful citizens, the idea that people are born to be either creative or lacking in creative ability, the notion that creativity is more a way of feeling than a way of thinking, the idea that creativity is something mysterious, and the notion that the word creativity applies to a simple, uncomplicated mental process that operates in unrestraint.

Mel Rhodes. "An Analysis of Creativity." *Phi Delta Kappa International.*

Chapter 12

Coda

Figure 12.1: Cover of Journal Number 106

Like many writers, I keep a journal and have been keeping journals since 1954. I write about my ideas, things I've purchased, topics I might want to consider writing about, and I illustrate them with my drawings.

When I am working on a book, not only do I write material for the book on my computer, but I also write about how the book is progressing in my journal, so there are two things going on: I'm writing a book and I'm writing in my journal about the book.

I often brainstorm in my journal and devote a page of my journal, in four columns, to the book. I also illustrate my journals with many drawings.

So, I can locate, in my journal, when I got the idea of writing choices. It was on Wednesday, December 28, 2022, on page 112 of journal 106. I wrote, "I wonder if I can do something about the sheer amount of choice available in consumer cultures.

Underneath that note, I wrote:

The Tyranny of
CHOICE
In American Consumer Culture
The God Shot (Espresso machines)
Blue Jeans, Nail Clippers, etc.

And beneath that I drew a four-column box in which I did some brainstorming on chapters I might write for the book. This box of ideas for a possible book is shown below.

Figure 12.2: Brainstorming on a Possible Book on Choices

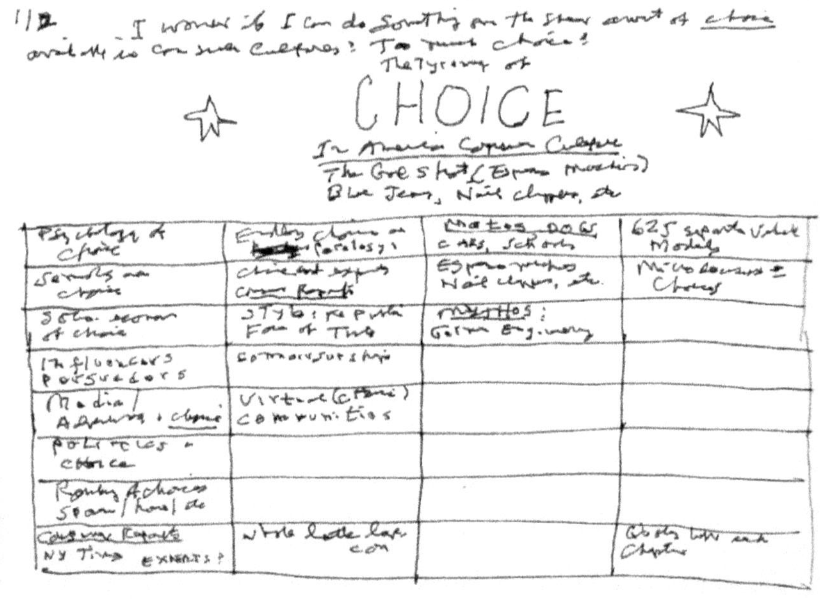

I became interested in the topic because, on September 20th, I purchased an inexpensive espresso machine and discovered an Internet organization, "Home Espresso Machine Aficionados," on Facebook that I joined.

The members of that organization posted notes about their problems in choosing what kind and brand of coffee grinders or espresso machines to get and related issues. That made me think about the dilemma of choices that members of the club faced.

As I thought about the book, I decided to devote a full page in my journal to brainstorming on a book on choices. I drew four lines to provide four columns to list topics and subjects that might be interesting to investigate and write about.

On various pages of the journal, I have parts of the page with three or four columns in which I brainstormed on some topic and played around with ideas.

Figure 12.3: Brainstorming Page on Choices

I should point out that I don't fill the page in one day but return to it as I think about the book and progress with it. On this page, I considered topics I would deal with, subjects to which I might devote a chapter and related concerns.

This brainstorming also reflects an element of my writing that is important. When I write a book, I see it as an investigation that I am conducting, so I never know how it will turn out. That is one of the reasons I like to offer quotations from writers and theorists whose ideas are important for my argument, so my readers can see what they had to say and how they expressed themselves.

If you think of a book as like a trial, the people whose ideas and quotes I offer can be thought of as witnesses for the defense, since my books are, in the final analysis, arguments about a topic that I am discussing.

There is also the matter of my writing style to consider and the appearance of my books. I write in a conversational, accessible style, even though I deal with very high-level thinkers in "esoteric" fields such as semiotics and psychoanalytic theory. As the notes in my Takeaways shows, readers of this book will have read material by Ferdinand de Saussure, Sigmund Freud, Karl Marx and many other important thinkers and theorists.

Books should have a visual appeal and so I include many drawings I've made of the theorists whose ideas I use and other images when possible. The drawings make the books more appealing and less daunting than if they had no images. I illustrate my journals with drawings and also illustrate my books to give them a friendlier and less intimidating look.

Le Mot Juste

There are around 30,000 words in this book. If you think about it, each word in the book is the result of a choice I made between it or some similar word. We can say the same thing about conversations with people. The French have a term, "Le Mot Juste," which means "the proper word" or "the correct word." When we speak, and when we write, we have many words to choose from, and each of those words conveys different meanings.

So, I had around 30,000-word choices to make, though in many cases, because of the nature of language, once I had chosen certain words, other words followed logically. To understand this better, it is a good idea to turn to the ideas of a Russian communication theorist, Mikhail Bakhtin and his ideas about the way texts are influenced by previously created texts.

Figure 12.4: Mikhail Bakhtin

Linguistic Theory: The Dialogic Aspects of Conversation

In a book of Bakhtin's writings (Michael Holquist, ed. Transl. Caryl Emerson and Michael Holquist), *The Dialogic Imagination: Four Essays by M.M. Bakhtin.* 1981, 279-281, published by the University of Texas Press, we read:

> The word is born in a dialogue as a living rejoinder with it; the world is shaped in dialogic interaction with an alien word that is already in the object. A word forms a concept of its own object in a dialogic way....The world in living conversation is directly, blatantly, oriented toward a future answer-word: it provokes an answer, anticipates it and structures itself in the answer's direction. Forming itself in an atmosphere of the already spoken, the word is at the same time determined by that which has not yet been said but which is needed and in fact anticipated by the answering world. Such is the case in any living dialogue.

> The linguistic significance of a given utterance is understood against the background of language, while its actual meaning is understood against the background of other concrete utterances on the same theme, a background made up of contradictory opinions, points of view and value judgments—that is, precisely that background that, as we see, complicates the path of any word toward its object. Only now this contradictory environment of alien words is present to the speaker not in the object, but rather in the consciousness of the listener

Mikhail Bakhtin (1875-1975) was an influential theorist of communication from Russia who has been "rediscovered" in the past several decades. He elaborated a theory of language called "dialogism," which focuses on the two-way aspects of communication—taking dialogue as its main metaphor for the communication process. It is an oversimplification to say that communication is dialogue, but not too far from the truth. Dialogue is basic to understanding communication, not monologue—in which we are talking to ourselves, so to speak.

So, when we speak with others, we must keep in mind what has already been said and anticipate what will be said. And this property is true of all discourse, of all kinds of communication in all media. That is, communication must consider cultural norms and beliefs and use them, just as it must consider future responses to that communication.

Bakhtin's dialogic perspective considers previous utterances and texts in all media, and implies another of Bakhtin's theories, one known as intertextuality. What this says, in brief, is that there are strong relationships between texts being produced at any moment in time and other texts that were previously produced. What we learn from Bakhtin is that the words we use are connected to the culture in which we are speaking and are tied to history, so to speak.

This means that my choice of words is connected to all kinds of things and is not innocent. When we use words, we must assume our listeners or readers know the codes that give them meaning. That means, when I'm writing, I want to make sure that my readers know the codes and can understand what I'm writing, which explains my accessible (as best I can) writing style.

Figure 12.5: Labyrinth

Juan Luis Borges wrote a famous short story, "The Garden of Forking Paths," about labyrinths, which does a wonderful job of suggesting the problems of choice, for in labyrinths we are constantly confronted with choices. In the myth, if you make the wrong choice, you end up encountering the minotaur. Here is a passage from the story:

> I know something about labyrinths. Not for nothing am I the great-grandson of Ts'ui Pen. He was Governor of Yunnan and gave up temporal power to write a novel with more characters than there are in the Hung Lou Meng, and to create a maze in which all men would lose themselves. He spent thirteen years on these oddly assorted tasks before he was assassinated by a stranger. His novel had no sense to it, and

nobody ever found his labyrinth. Under the trees of England, I meditated on this lost and perhaps mythical labyrinth. I imagined it untouched and perfect on the secret summit of some mountain; I imagined it drowned under rice paddies or beneath the sea; I imagined it infinite, made not only of eight-sided pavilions and of twisting paths but also of rivers, provinces and kingdoms....I thought of a maze of mazes, of a sinuous, ever growing maze which would take in both past and future and would somehow involve the stars. Lost in these imaginary illusions, I forgot my destiny - that of the hunted. For an undetermined period of time, I felt myself cut off from the world, an abstract spectator. The hazy and murmuring countryside, the moon, the decline of the evening, stirred within me. Going down the gently sloping road I could not feel fatigue. The evening was at once intimate and infinite.

This is one of the most famous stories by Borges, and its title suggests the dilemma we all face as we move through life, where "forking paths," that is, choices, continually confront us.

I hope that this book on choices will have given you some ideas about the role of choices in our lives, our society, our culture and our politics (among other things) and that you will be more mindful of the choices you make about both mundane and trivial matters and about significant and life shaping/life changing choices as well.

Arthur Asa Berger
Mill Valley, California

Glossary

Aberrant Decoding. The notion, elaborated by the Italian semiotician Umberto Eco, is that audiences decode or interpret texts such as television commercials and print advertisements in ways that differ from the ways the creators of these texts expect them to be decoded. Aberrant decoding is the rule rather than the exception when it comes to the mass media, according to Eco. It has been estimated that about 25% of advertisements and commercials are decoded aberrantly.

Adam and Eve in the Garden. Adam and Eve, the first man and woman created by God in his own image, lived in the **Garden of Eden**, where God provided for their needs as long as they did not eat from the tree of the knowledge of good and evil. They were tempted by the serpent, who lied to them that eating from the tree would make them like God. They disobeyed God and ate the fruit, which led to their banishment from the Garden and the introduction of sin and death to the human race. They are the ancestors of all humankind and a central story in the Judeo-Christian and Islamic traditions.

Addiction. This term, as used in the book, describes a dependency and kind of compulsive behavior people develop about their iPhones, video games they like, and digitally accessed material of all kinds. It is also applied to drugs. An addiction is a chronic dysfunction of the brain system that involves reward, motivation, and memory. It's about the way your body craves a substance or behavior, especially if it causes a compulsive or obsessive pursuit of "reward" and a lack of concern over consequences. Someone experiencing an addiction will be unable to stay away from the substance or stop the addictive behavior, display a lack of self-control, have an increased desire for the substance or behavior, dismiss how their behavior may be causing problems, and lack an emotional response.

https://www.healthline.com/health/addiction

Advertisement. The word "advert" means "to call attention to something," and thus, an advertisement is, for our purposes, a kind of text—carried by electronic or print media—that attracts attention to, stimulates a desire for, and sometimes leads to the purchase of a product or service. The convention is that commercial messages in print are called advertisements and those in electronic media are called commercials.

Alienation. In Marxist theory, capitalist societies can create enormous amounts of consumer goods, but they also inevitably generate alienation and feelings of estrangement from oneself and others in society. Alienation is functional for those who own the means of production and distribution since alienation leads to consumer cultures—ones characterized by endless and frantic consumption, which people use as an escape from their feelings of alienation. In capitalist societies, therefore, advertising plays a central role in maintaining the status quo and distracting people from focusing attention on the inequality found in capitalist countries.

Anomie. Durkheim used the term to describe people who don't abide by the norms that most people have in a society. The "a" in the word means "no" and the "nomie" means norms. Anomie differs from alienation. Members of a gang may be anomic, but they aren't suffering from alienation. Émile Durkheim (1858-1917) was the first to put forth the concept of anomie. It is a state of extreme social disorganization or a "normless condition." It is characterized by deviance in human behavior and the breakdown of norms. Anomie arises when there are few social expectations to guide behavior.

Apple iPhone. This phone became an international bestseller when it was introduced and remains one of the most popular smartphones.

Aristotle. Aristotle, Greek Aristoteles (born 384 BCE in Stagira, Chalcidice, Greece—died 322, Chalcis, Euboea), was an ancient Greek philosopher and scientist, one of the greatest intellectual figures of Western history. His writings cover many subjects, including physics, biology, zoology, metaphysics, logic, poetry, theatre, music, rhetoric, psychology, linguistics, economics, politics, meteorology, geology, and government.

Audience. Audiences are defined as collections of individuals who watch a television program, listen to a radio show, watch a film, spend time on social media or spend time at some kind of live artistic performance (symphony, rock band concert, and so on). The members of the audience may be together in one room or, in the case of television, each watching from his or her own set. In technical communication terms, audiences are addressees who receive mediated texts sent by an addresser. In conversations, an audience can be one person.

Borges, Juan Luis. He was born on August 24, 1899, in Buenos Aires, Argentina, and died in Geneva, Switzerland on June 14, 1986. Borges was an Argentine poet, essayist, and short-story writer whose works became classics of twentieth-century world literature. His best-known books, F*iccio*nes *(Fictions)* and *El Aleph (The Aleph)*, published in the 1940s, are collections of short stories.

Bourdieu, Pierre. He was an influential French sociologist who argued that taste is tied to our socioeconomic status or our economic and cultural capital and is shaped more by social forces than personal desires or preferences. His book, *Distinction,* is considered one of the most important books by a sociologist in recent decades. His theory of the habitus argues that the earliest experiences of children in their families play an important role in their development.

Brands. Brands create emotional ties between individuals and certain products or services who often will purchase them throughout their lives. From a semiotic perspective, brands are signs people used to display their taste or wealth and to help fashion an identity. The fact that certain companies prominently attach their logos to their products helps purchasers of these products to secure their identities.

Butler, Judith. A leading feminist thinker and the author of an influential book, *Gender Trouble and the Subversion of Identity.* Butler argues that gender is a performance and that the bipolar opposition of male and female is no longer valid. Butler is a professor of rhetoric and comparative literature at the University of California at Berkeley.

Buyer's Remorse. "Buyer's remorse refers to negative emotions—such as regret, anxiety or guilt—that consumers may experience after buying an item. It's typically linked to large purchases—like a car or a new home. But some people may experience it after smaller purchases—like buying a new bag or set of golf clubs. A person could experience buyer's remorse for a number of different reasons. For example, impulse buys or overspending could cause a consumer to regret their purchase. A new homebuyer may worry they missed out on something better on the market. Others might feel like they made the wrong decision or didn't do enough research before buying. Whatever the reason, buyer's remorse is something many people may feel at some point in their lives. In fact, a recent Bankrate survey found that 64% of millennials are now second-guessing their recent home purchases. Many of these first-time homeowners cited unexpected maintenance costs and spending at the top end of their budgets as the main reasons for their remorse."

"What is the buyers remorse? And how to avoid it." September 27, 2022. *Capital One.* https://www.capitalone.com/learn-grow/money-management/buyers-remorse/

Celebrity. A celebrity is someone who is well known by people for reasons that are difficult to determine. Celebrities often play a role as influencers in shaping people's consumption practices. The lives of celebrities are publicly consumed as dramatic entertainment, and their commercial brand is made profitable for those who exploit their popularity.

Certeau, Michel de. Michel de Certeau (1925-1986) was a French Jesuit priest, philosopher, and scholar who is best known for his work in the fields of cultural studies, history, and philosophy. Certeau is considered to be one of the most influential thinkers of the twentieth century. His most famous work is *The Practice of Everyday Life,* a book that explores the ways in which individuals subvert dominant systems and structures through everyday practices of resistance. In this work, de Certeau argues that individuals, through their everyday actions and practices, create their own unique cultural and social meanings, even within the confines of larger, more oppressive systems.

Chandler, Daniel. A contemporary British semiotician and author of a well-known book on semiotics, *Semiotics: The Basics,* now in its fourth edition. He has written a great deal on codes and their relation to signs in semiotic theory and is also interested in visual semiotics and other aspects of communication.

Choice. Since the mid-twentieth century, the term choice has been operationally defined in a variety of different ways in psychology. Choice has often been studied as the outcome of a decision-making process. Economic theories of rational choice assume both that the decisions individuals make will determine their behavior and that decisions will be made based on a general set of rational laws. Britannica explains it this way: choice, in philosophy, the supposed ability to freely decide between alternatives. Choice is a corollary of the traditional notion of free will, understood as the supposed power or capacity of humans to make decisions or perform actions independently of any prior event in or state of the universe.

Claritas. A market research company that provides consumer insights and segmentation analysis to businesses. The company was founded in 1971 and is based in Chicago, Illinois. Claritas uses a variety of data sources and analytical techniques to help businesses better understand their target markets and consumer behavior. This information can be used to develop marketing strategies, improve product offerings, and make informed business decisions. Claritas is known for its PRIZM segmentation system, which categorizes U.S. households into 68 distinct lifestyle segments based on demographic and behavioral data. It suggests that many of its categories live in the same zip code areas, arguing that "birds of a feather flock together."

Class. From a linguistic standpoint, a class is any group of things that have something in common. We use the term to refer to social classes, or more literally, socioeconomic classes: groups of people who share income and lifestyle. Marxist theorists argue that there is a ruling class, which shapes the ideas of the proletariat, the working class. Advertisers are interested in socioeconomic classes and lifestyles because these phenomena are held to be the key to selling products and services. Marxists argue that there is a ruling class in capitalist societies that shapes people's thinking about politics and many other areas.

Codes. Codes are systems of symbols, letters, words, sounds, whatever generates meaning. Language, for example, is a code. It uses combinations of letters that we call words to mean certain things. The relation between the word and the thing the word stands for is arbitrary, based on convention. Sometimes, the term code is used to describe hidden meanings and disguised communications. Semioticians explain that people must know certain codes if they are to interpret signs correctly. Daniel Chandler explains in his book, *Semiotics: The Basics*, that "the meaning of a sign depends on the code within which it is situated, codes provide a framework within which signs make sense."

Collective Representations. The French sociologist Emile Durkheim used this concept to deal with the fact that people are both individuals pursuing their own aims and social animals guided by the groups and societies in which they find themselves. Collective representations are, broadly speaking, texts that reflect the beliefs and ideals of collectivities.

Communication. There are many ways of understanding and using this term. For our purposes, communication is a process that involves the transmission of messages from senders to receivers. We often distinguish between communication using language, verbal communication, and communication using non-verbal communication, such as facial expressions and body language. Another definition of communication is that it involves exchanging information or ideas between two or more individuals or entities. It can take many forms, including verbal or written communication, body language, gestures, facial expressions, and other nonverbal cues. Effective communication is essential for personal and professional relationships, as well as for business and other organizations. It can help build trust, resolve conflicts, and promote understanding. There are many factors that can affect the effectiveness of communication, such as language barriers, cultural differences, misunderstandings, and emotions.

Consumer Cultures. Consumer cultures are characterized by widespread personal consumption rather than socially conscious and useful investment in the public sphere. The focus is on private expenditure and leisure pursuits, and this leads to privatism, self-centeredness, and a reluctance to allocate resources to the public realm. Advertising is held by many critics to be a primary instrument of those who own the means of production in generating consumer lust and consumer cultures and distracting people from social and public matters. Social scientists Aaron Wildavsky and Mary Douglas suggest that there are four political cultures, that also function as consumer cultures: hierarchical or elitist, individualist, egalitarian, and fatalist. Luxury goods make up about 10% of purchases in consumer cultures.

Culture. Culture refers to the shared beliefs, values, customs, behaviors, and artifacts that characterize a group or society. It includes everything from language, religion, and traditions to food, clothing, and art. Culture is shaped by a wide range of factors, such as geography, history, economics, politics, and social structures. It is a dynamic and ever-changing entity that develops over time and is often subject to outside influences and internal conflicts. Understanding and respecting cultural differences is crucial for promoting social harmony and global cooperation and for avoiding misunderstandings and conflicts. It involves the transmission from generation to generation of specific ideas, arts, customary beliefs, ways of living, behavior patterns, institutions, and values. When applied to the arts, or "elite culture," it is used to specify "elite" kinds of artworks, such as operas, poetry, classical music, and serious art. Postmodernists do not consider "elite" culture and "popular culture" to differ significantly from one another.

Culture Code. The title of a book by Clotaire Rapaille that describes consumption practices in different countries. It argues that children, up to the age of seven, become imprinted by a particular country's codes of behavior and taste and that these codes shape people's behavior for the rest of their lives. I argue in many of my writings that what we think of as a culture can be understood to be a collection of codes of behavior and thinking that people learn while growing up in a culture or subculture. If you understand people's codes, you can better understand their behavior.

Cultural Studies aka Cultural Criticism. The term "cultural criticism" refers to the analysis of texts and various aspects of everyday life by scholars in various disciplines who use concepts from their fields of expertise to interpret mass-mediated texts, the role of the mass media, and related concerns. The focus is on what impact these texts and the media that carry them have on individuals, society, and culture. Cultural criticism involves the use of literary theory, media analysis, philosophical thought, communication theory, and various interpretive methodologies, such as semiotics, psychoanalytic theory, Marxist theory, and sociological theory.

Defense Mechanisms. According to Freudian psychoanalytic theory, defense mechanisms are methods used by the ego to defend itself against pressures from the id or impulsive elements in the psyche and the superego, such as conscience and guilt. Some of the more common defense mechanisms are *repression* (barring unconscious instinctual wishes, memories, and so on from consciousness), *regression* (returning to earlier stages in one's development), *ambivalence* (a simultaneous feeling of love and hate for a person, thing or concept), and *rationalization* (offering excuses to justify one's actions).

Demographics. The term refers to similarities found in groups of people in terms of race, religion, gender, social class, ethnicity, occupation, place of residence, age, and so on. Demographic information plays an important role in creating advertising and the choice of which media to use to deliver this advertising.

Disfunctional or Dysfunctional. In sociological thought, something is disfunctional if it contributes to the breakdown or destabilization of the entity in which it is found. Functional theory is one of the dominant concerns of many sociologists, political scientists, and social scientists. (See Functional.)

Dialogism. According to Mikhail Bakhtin, dialogism describes the process in which meaning is developed out of interactions among the author, the work, and the reader or listener. Also, these elements are affected by the contexts in which they are placed, namely by social and political forces. It can also be described as a principle or condition of interconnecting performative differences underpinning all forms of communication. We cannot understand how meaning is produced, Bakhtin argues, unless we recognize that the meaning of individual words is the result of a negotiation, not only between actual speakers in dialogue with one another but also with language itself. All language users shift and reshape the meaning of words according to the demands of their situation.

Maria Shevtsova. 1992. Dialogism in the Novel and Bakhtin's Theory of Culture. *New Literary History*, 23(3), 747-763.

Douglas, Mary. A British social anthropologist who developed grid-group theory, which argues that the number of rules and restrictions and the boundaries of the "lifestyles" to which people belong shapes their preferences in many areas. These lifestyles are not self-conscious groups but exist in modern societies and affect people's taste, politics, and many other areas of life. In an influential article, "In Defence of Shopping," she explained, "We must make a radical shift away from thinking about consumption as a manifestation of individual choices. Culture itself is the result of myriads of individual choices, not primarily between commodities but between kinds of relationships."

Durkheim, Emile. Durkheim (1858-1917), one of the most important sociologists, is considered the father of French sociology. He is the author of a classic study of suicide, of religion, and numerous other books. Durkheim is one of the most influential functionalist theorists. He argued that social solidarity is achieved through shared values and beliefs, and that social order is maintained through social control and regulation.

Eco, Umberto. (1932-2016) An influential Italian semiotician and novelist whose work on semiotic theory and its application to popular culture and other kinds of texts and phenomena have been very important. His extremely complex novels are popular in Europe and many other countries. His novel, *Name of the Rose* was made into a popular film.

Edwards, Jonathan. Jonathan Edwards (1703-1758) was an American theologian, preacher, and philosopher who is considered to be one of the greatest Protestant theologians and intellectuals in American history. He was born in East Windsor, Connecticut, and grew up in a Puritan family. Edwards was educated at Yale University and later became a minister in Northampton, Massachusetts. Edwards is best known for his sermon, "Sinners in the Hands of an Angry God," which he delivered in 1741 during the Great Awakening, a period of religious revival in the American colonies. The sermon warned listeners of the eternal consequences of sin and the importance of repentance and conversion. When it comes to choices and free will, Edwards argued that man can act as he pleases but not please as he pleases, thus allowing free will in humans and, allowing God to be all powerful.

Egalitarians. They stress that everyone is equal in terms of certain needs, such as food, shelter, and access to health care. Egalitarians function as critics of the two dominant political/consumer cultures—elitist and individualist. Egalitarians are one of the four "lifestyles" discussed by social-anthropologist Mary Douglas and grid-group theorists.

Ego. In Sigmund Freud's theory of the psyche, the ego functions as the executor of the id and as a mediator between the id and the superego (conscience). The ego is involved in the perception of reality and adaptation to reality.

Ekman, Paul. American psychologist and world-famous authority on facial expression. He is one of the most important psychologists in recent years.

Enclavists. Mary Douglas' term for Egalitarians. Enclavists are one of the four lifestyles Douglas wrote about in her work on grid-group theory.

Erikson, Erik. (1902-1994) He was a developmental psychoanalyst who wrote important studies of children and adolescents. Erikson was born in Germany but practiced in America and is considered one of the most important psychologists in recent years. He argued that personality develops in a predetermined order through eight stages of psychosocial development, from infancy to adulthood.

Ethnomethodology. This branch of sociology deals with how social interactions shape the social order. It is interested in analyzing conversation as a key to understanding behavior. Harold Garfinkel was one of its most outstanding theorists.

False Consciousness. In Marxist thought, false consciousness refers to mistaken ideas that people have about their class, status, and economic possibilities. These ideas help maintain the status quo and are of great use to members of the ruling class who want to avoid changes in the social and economic structure of a society. Karl Marx argued that the ideas of the ruling class are always the ruling ideas in society. Marxists would argue that the belief many Americans have that they can succeed if they have enough willpower and are "elites" because they can consume at a relatively high level, are examples of false consciousness.

Fatalists. They are at the bottom rungs of society—they have little political or consumer power and can only escape their status as a result of luck or chance, such as winning a lottery. Fatalists are one of the four "lifestyles" discussed by grid-group theorists.

Feminist Theory. Feminist theory focuses on the roles given to women and the way they are portrayed in texts of all kinds, including one of the worst offenders—advertising. Feminist critics argue that women are typically used as sexual objects and are portrayed stereotypically in advertisements and other kinds of texts, and this has negative effects on both men and women.

Functional. In sociological thought, the term "functional" refers to the contributions something makes to the maintenance of society or an institution or entity. Many social scientists are functionalists. (See Disfunctional, Dysfunctional.)

Functional Alternative. This term refers to something that takes the place of something else. For example, professional football can be seen as a functional alternative to religion. I argue that department stores can be seen as a modern functional alternative to medieval cathedrals.

Gans, Herbert. An American sociologist who has written about popular culture in America and argues that there are what he calls "taste cultures" that are appropriate for different socio-economic classes.

Gender. Gender is the sexual category of an individual, male or female, and the behavioral traits that relate to each category. Gender is now held to be "socially constructed," which means it is our societies that determine what we think about gender. The binary distinction between males and females is no longer considered valid by many people and individuals now have a range of possibilities when defining their gender.

GOP: The "Grand Old Party," which is another name for the Republican Party, has changed in recent years and become more ideologically extreme, and some would argue, a cult dominated by Donald Trump.

Gorer, Geoffrey. Geoffrey Gorer (1905-1985) was an English anthropologist, sociologist, and writer best known for his studies of sexuality, cultural norms, and social structures. He was a prolific author who wrote extensively on a variety of topics, including anthropology, psychology, and cultural studies. Gorer's work often focused on the intersection between culture and human behavior, and he was particularly interested in understanding how cultural values and beliefs shape individual and collective attitudes towards sex, death, and other taboo subjects. One of Gorer's most famous works is "The Pornography of Death," a controversial essay in which he argued that Western societies have an unhealthy fascination with death and that this obsession is reflected in the media and popular culture. Other notable works by Gorer include "Exploring English Character," "The American People," and "Death, Grief, and Mourning in Contemporary Britain."

Grid-Group Theory. This theory is based on the work of social anthropologist Mary Douglas, who argued that there are four (and only four) consumer cultures or "lifestyles" in modern societies based on the degree to which the groups have weak or strong boundaries and whether members have few or many rules and prescriptions to follow. The four antagonistic lifestyles compete with one another but also need each other.

Habitus. This concept deals with the impact of early childhood experiences on people's development. Bourdieu defines it as "a subjective but not individual system of internalized structures, schemes of perception, conception, and action common to all members of the same group or class."

Haug, Wolfgang. A German Marxist who has written extensively about consumer culture and the role of aesthetics in advertising and marketing.

Hierarchical Elitists. These people are one of the four lifestyles in grid-group theory and are at the top of the economic and power pyramid. They believe hierarchy is needed for society to run smoothly. They also have a sense of obligation to those beneath them. Elitists and individualists make up the core of luxury purchasers since they have the social and economic capital needed to buy luxury products and services.

Hypothesis. A hypothesis is a guess about something. Social scientists use the term to suggest that they have ideas that may be interesting and even correct but which they have not been able to verify. We use the term to signify that we have an interesting idea about something but lack proof that our idea is correct.

Id. The Id in Freud's theory of the psyche (technically known as his structural hypothesis) is that element of the psyche that is the representative of a person's drives. In *New Introductory Lectures on Psychoanalysis*, Freud called it "a chaos, a cauldron of seething excitement." It also is the source of energy, but lacks direction and needs the ego to harness it and control it. In popular thought, it is connected to impulse, lust, and "I want it all now" behavior. Many advertisements for all kinds of products and services appeal to Id elements in our psyches.

Ideology. An ideology is a logically coherent, integrated explanation of social, economic, and political matters that helps establish the goals and direct the actions of a group or political entity. People act (and vote or don't vote) based on an ideology they hold, even though they may not have articulated it or thought about it. Some critics argue that advertising is an ideological tool that members of the ruling class use to distract the proletariat from their problems and convince them that the political order is worth supporting.

Image. Defining images is extremely difficult. In my book, *Seeing Is Believing: An Introduction to Visual Communication,* I define an image as "a collection of signs and symbols—what we find when we look at a photograph, a film still, a shot of a television screen, a print advertisement, or just about anything." The term is used for mental as well as physical representations of things. Images often have powerful emotional effects on people and historical significance.

Imprints. According to the French psychoanalyst and marketing theorist Clotaire Rapaille, children in all countries are imprinted, by the age of seven, by the culture of the country in which they grow up. These imprints then shape, to a considerable degree, their thinking and behavior when they are adults. He discusses this in his book, *Culture Codes.*

Individualists. In Grid-Group theory, individualists are members of a lifestyle that believes that the basic function of government is to prevent crime and invasion by foreign powers. They are competitive and stress the importance of individual initiative.

Intertextuality. This theory argues that texts (works of art) of all kinds are influenced to varying degrees by texts that preceded them. Sometimes, as in the case of parody, the relationship is overt, but in many cases, creators of texts are influenced by stylistic practices or thematic ones from earlier works. We can say, then, that intertextuality involves alluding to, imitating, modifying, or adapting previously created texts and styles of expression. Parody is a literary style that is intertextual. Some examples of intertextuality are Disney's *The Lion King* which is a take on Shakespeare's *Hamlet* and J.K. Rowling's *Harry Potter* series, which makes use of T.H. White's *The Sword in the Stone*, and C. S. Lewis's *The Chronicles of Narnia.*

Isolates. The term Mary Douglas used for the lifestyle described by others as Fatalists.

Jameson, Fredric. He is one of the most important theorists of postmodernism and the author of an influential book, *Postmodernism, or, The Cultural Logic of Late Capitalism.* Jameson argues that postmodernism should be seen as an advanced form of capitalism.

Latent Functions. Latent functions are hidden, unrecognized, and unintended results of some activity, entity, or institution. Latent functions are contrasted by social scientists with manifest functions, which are recognized and intended. The manifest function of buying a luxury automobile may be because it is technically superior to other cars, but the latent function of buying the car is to show that one can afford it and to gain status.

Lifestyle. Literally, style of life. Lifestyle refers to the way people live—to the decisions they make about how to decorate their homes (and where the homes are located), the cars they drive, the clothes they wear, the foods they eat, the restaurants they visit, and where they go for vacations. Lifestyles tend to be coherent or logically connected, and they play an important part in market research because lifestyles shape consumption patterns in individuals. Social anthropologist Mary Douglas, in an article on shopping, uses the term to describe the four kinds of consumers found in contemporary societies: elitists, individualists, egalitarians, and fatalists. She argues that people's lifestyles play an important role in determining their preferences in many areas of life in consumption cultures.

LGBTQIA+. These letters stand for Lesbian, Gay, Bisexual, Transgender, Queer/Questioning, Intersexual, Asexual/Aromantic, and other identities in Queerness—all of which are possibilities in non-binary gender identities. It is used to refer to individuals and communities that identify with these diverse sexual orientations and gender identities. The acronym has been expanded over time to be more inclusive, with variations such as LGBTQIA (adding Intersex and Asexual), LGBTQIA+ (adding additional identities), or simply "queer" as an umbrella term. It is important to recognize and respect the diversity of experiences within the LGBTQ+ community.

Manifest Functions. The manifest functions of an activity, entity, or institution are those that are obvious and intended. Manifest functions contrast with latent functions, which are hidden and unintended. The manifest function of advertising is to sell products and services; the latent function is to sell the political order. (See also Latent Functions.)

Mass Communication. This term refers to the transfer of messages, information, and texts from a sender to many receivers, forming a mass audience. This transfer is done through the technologies of the mass media—newspapers, magazines, television programs, films, records, computers, the Internet, and CD-ROMs. A sender is often a person in a large media organization, the messages are public, and the audience tends to be large and varied. With the development of social media such as Facebook and Instagram, many individuals can now communicate with large numbers of people.

Medium (plural: Media). A medium is a means of delivering messages, information, or texts to audiences. There are different ways of classifying the media. One of the most common ways is print (newspapers, magazines, books, billboards), electronic (radio, television, computers, CD-ROMs, the Internet), and photographic (photographs, films, videos). Various critics have suggested that the primary function of the commercial media is to deliver audiences to advertisers and that everything else the media does is of secondary importance.

Metaphor. A metaphor is a figure of speech that conveys meaning by analogy. For example, "My love is a rose." It is important to realize that metaphors are not confined to poetry and literary works but, according to some linguists, are the fundamental way in which we make sense of things and find meaning in the world. A simile is a weaker form of metaphor that uses either "like" or "as" in making an analogy. Metaphors are an important element in advertising. For example, Fidji perfume had a campaign that was explicitly metaphorical: "Woman is an island.' If the advertisement had said, "Woman is like an island," that would have been a simile.

Metonymy. According to linguists, metonymy is a figure of speech that conveys information by association and is, along with metaphor, one of the most important ways people send information to one another. We tend not to be aware of our use of metonymy, but whenever we use association to get an idea about something (Rolls-Royce signifies wealth), we are thinking metonymically. A form of metonymy that involves seeing a whole in terms of a part, or vice versa, is called synecdoche. Using the Pentagon to stand for the American military is an example of synecdoche. Metonymy is an important technique used by advertisers to generate emotional responses to advertisements in people.

Modernism. The period before postmodernism, from roughly 1900 to 1960, before postmodernism became culturally dominant. Modernism's esthetics and values, its belief in master narratives (like its belief in progress), and grand theories were rejected by postmodernist thinkers and people affected by postmodernist thought.

Myth. Myths are conventionally understood to be sacred stories about gods and cultural heroes (and, in more recent years, mass-mediated heroes and heroines) that are used to transmit a culture's basic belief system to younger generations and to explain natural and supernatural phenomena. *Choices* argues that myths play an important role in shaping our behavior in many areas of life, which I describe as the "myth model."

Myth Model. This model suggests that myths inform many aspects of our lives, though we may not recognize this is the case. It shows how myths can be found in psychoanalytic theory, historical experience, elite culture, popular culture, and everyday life.

National character. This theory argues that people who grow up in a country can be characterized by certain values, beliefs, and distinctive behaviors. Thus, there is a big difference between people in different countries—a topic explored by Clotaire Rapaille in his book, *The Culture Code,* and the work of the anthropologist Geoffrey Gorer along with countless others.

Nonfunctional. In sociological thought, something is nonfunctional if it is neither functional nor dysfunctional and plays no role in the entity in which it is found.

Nonverbal Communication. Our body language, facial expressions, styles of dress, and hairstyles are examples of our communicating feelings and attitudes (and a sense of who we are) without words. In our everyday lives, a great deal of our communication is done nonverbally. It is estimated that between 60-90% of the messages we send to others are nonverbal in nature.

Ocean Cruising. It is an increasingly important form of tourism, with lines that appeal to people of different incomes and tastes. Cruises can cost as little as $50 a day per person to $1000 a day or more per person on some luxury liners and specialty excursion ships.

Pappenheim, Fritz. A German Marxist who wrote about the importance of alienation in Marxist theory and the impact of alienation on life in capitalist countries.

Peirce, Charles Sanders. (1839-1914) One of the founding fathers of the study of signs who gave the science its name, semiotics, a term based on the Greek word for sign, sēmeîon. He was a professor at Harvard and produced many seminal works on semiotic theory.

Phallic Symbol. In Freudian theory, an object that resembles the penis either by shape or function is described as a phallic symbol. Symbolism is a defense mechanism of the ego that permits hidden or repressed sexual or aggressive thoughts to be expressed in a disguised form. For a discussion of this topic, see Freud's book, *An Interpretation of Dreams.* I offer the example of the Washington Monument as a gigantic phallic symbol named after the father of our country.

Phallocentric. The term phallocentric is used to suggest societies that are dominated by males, and the ultimate source of this domination, which shapes our institutions and cultures, is the male phallus. In this theory, a link is made between male sexuality and male power.

Pines, Maya. American journalist and author of an article on semiotics discussed in this book. She explained that what semioticians call signs should be seen as messages conveying meaning and that people are always sending signs about themselves and interpreting signs others send to them.

Popular. "Popular" is one of the most difficult terms used in discourse about the arts and the media. The term means "appealing to many people." It comes from the Latin *popularis,* which means "of the people." Separating the popular and elite arts has become increasingly problematic in recent years, and the idea that they are radically different has been rejected by postmodern theorists. For example, is an opera shown on television an example of elite or popular culture?

Popular Culture. Popular culture is a term that identifies certain kinds of texts, generally mass-mediated, that appeal to many people. But mass communication theorists often identify "popular" with "mass" and suggest that if something is popular, it must be of poor quality, appealing to the mythical "lowest common denominator." Popular culture is generally held to be the opposite of elite culture—arts that require certain levels of sophistication and refinement to be appreciated, such as ballet, opera, poetry, and classical music. Many critics now question this popular culture/elite culture polarity.

Postmodernism. This theory states that a new kind of culture has developed in the United States and elsewhere since approximately 1960. It rejects the values and beliefs of the modernist society that had been dominant until that time. One theorist of postmodernism argued that it involves "incredulity toward metanarratives," by which he means the rejection of the overarching religious, social, political, aesthetic, and moral theories of the modernist period that had shaped people's thinking and their lives. Postmodernism is associated with stylistic eclecticism and a rejection of the split between elite and popular culture. The theory is very controversial, and important facets of it are explored in my books *Postmortem for a Postmodernist* (a postmodern mystery) and *The Portable Postmodernist.*

Psychoanalytic Theory. Sigmund Freud can be said to be the founding father of psychoanalytic theory. He argued that the human psyche had three levels: consciousness, preconsciousness, and the unconscious, which is the largest area of the psyche and an area not able to be accessed by individuals. What is important, psychoanalytic theorists argue, is that the unconscious shapes and affects our mental functioning and our behavior. Another of his theories posited three forces in the psyche: the id (desire), the ego (reason), and the superego (guilt), which were continually battling with one another for domination. Freud believed that sexuality and what he called "the Oedipus

Complex" play a dominant role in human behavior, even if their presence is not recognized.

Psychographics In marketing, the term psychographics is used to deal with groups of people who have similar psychological characteristics or profiles. It differs from demographics, which marketers use to focus on social and economic characteristics that people have in common.

QAnon. At its heart, QAnon is a wide-ranging, unfounded theory that says that former president Donald J. Trump is waging a secret war against elite Satan-worshipping pedophiles in government, business, and the media. QAnon believers think that this fight will lead to a day of reckoning, when many prominent people (mostly Democrats), such as former presidential candidate Hillary Clinton, will be arrested and executed.

Rapaille, Clotaire. French psychoanalyst and marketer who wrote *The Culture Code* and *The Global Code,* which deal with how different nationalities and new global elites shape purchasing decisions. He argued that children up to the age of seven are imprinted with the meaning of things most central to their lives and that different countries imprint different codes on children.

Rationalization. In Freudian thought, rationalization is a defense mechanism of the ego that creates an excuse to justify an action (or inaction when an action is expected). Ernest Jones, who introduced the term, used it to describe logical and rational reasons that people give to justify behavior that is really caused by unconscious and irrational determinants. We often use rationalizations to justify purchases that are unwise and unnecessary.

Riviera, Joan. She was a British psychoanalyst and a founding member of the British Psychoanalytical Society. In addition, she was an editor of *The International Journal of Psycho-Analysis* from 1920 until 1937. Riviera translated Freud's work into English and co-authored a book with another British psychoanalyst, Melanie Klein, *Love, Hate and Reparation.* Riviere's contribution to the book was titled "Hate, Greed and Aggression." The book is based on public lectures given in March 1936 about "The Emotional Life of Civilized Men and Women."

Role. Sociologists describe a role as a way of behavior that we learn in a society and that is appropriate to a particular situation. A person generally plays many roles with different people during the hours of a day, such as parent (family), worker (job), and spouse (marriage). We also use the term to describe the parts actors have in mass-mediated texts, including commercials.

Rubinstein, Ruth P. American sociologist of fashion and clothing and author of *Dress Codes: Meaning and Messages in American Culture.* The book uses semiotic and sociological theory to understand various aspects of fashion.

Sapirstein, Milton. American psychiatrist who has written about the psychological significance of different aspects of everyday life such as furnishing an apartment and the psychological and cultural significance of sex manuals.

Semiotics. Literally, the term means "the science of signs." Sēmeîon is the Greek term for sign; a sign as being anything that can be used to stand for something else. According to C. S. Peirce, one of the founders of the science, a sign "is something which stands to somebody for something in some respect or capacity." Semiotics is one of the core disciplines used by cultural studies scholars.

Schopenhauer, Arthur. (1788-1860) A German philosopher known for his pessimistic view of the world and his emphasis on the importance of individual will. He was deeply influenced by Eastern philosophy, particularly Buddhism, and believed that the goal of human life was to escape the cycle of suffering through the renunciation of desires and the attainment of inner peace. Schopenhauer's most famous work is "The World as Will and Representation," in which he argued that the universe is fundamentally characterized by an irrational force called the "will to live," which is responsible for all human and animal behavior. According to Schopenhauer, this will is insatiable and can never be fully satisfied, leading to an endless cycle of desire and suffering. Schopenhauer also believed that art, particularly music, was a powerful means of escaping the suffering of the world and connecting with a higher spiritual reality. He was a major influence on later philosophers, such as Friedrich Nietzsche and Sigmund Freud.

Sign. The basic concept in semiotics, the science of signs (from the Greek word sēmeîon, sign), that deals with how we find meaning in images and other kinds of communication. Ferdinand de Saussure, one of the founding fathers of semiotics, argued that a sign is made up of a *signifier* (a sound or object) and a *signified* (a concept). The relation between the signifier and the signified is arbitrary and not natural. C. S. Peirce, another founding father of semiotics, had a different notion. He said a sign is "something which stands to somebody for something in some respect or capacity." His theory of signs is dealt with in the discussion of symbols.

Simmel, Georg. (1858-1918) A German sociologist and philosopher who wrote on culture and society and whose ideas led to the development of urban sociology. Because he was Jewish, he never got a chair in an important German university, but his writings have been very influential, especially for non-positivist sociologists.

Social Control. Social controls are ideas, beliefs, values, and mores people get from their societies that shape their beliefs and behavior. People are both individuals with certain distinctive physical and emotional characteristics and desires and members of societies who are shaped to a certain degree by the institutions found in these societies.

Socialization. Socialization refers to the processes by which societies teach individuals how to behave: what rules to obey, roles to assume, and values to hold. Socialization was traditionally done by the family, educators, religious figures, and peers. The mass media, in general and advertising, in particular, seem to have usurped this function to a considerable degree nowadays, with consequences that are not always positive.

Socioeconomic Class. A socioeconomic class is a categorization of people according to their incomes and related social status and lifestyles. In Marxist thought, there are ruling classes that shape the consciousness of the working classes, and history is, in essence, a record of class conflict.

Spectacle. The focus on spectacle is found in the book *The Society of the Spectacle* by Guy Debord. He argues that capitalist societies are shaped by spectacles and the triumph of images and illusions over reality.

Stereotypes. Stereotypes are commonly held, simplistic, and inaccurate group portraits of categories of people. Stereotypes can be positive, negative, or mixed, but generally, they are negative. Stereotyping involves making gross overgeneralizations. (All Mexicans, Chinese, Jews, African Americans, WASPS, Americans, lawyers, doctors, professors, and so on are held to have certain characteristics, usually negative.)

Subculture. Any complex society comprises many subcultures that differ from the dominant culture in terms of such matters as ethnicity, race, religion, sexual orientation, beliefs, values, and tastes. Often, members of subcultures are marginalized and victimized by members of the dominant culture.

Superego. In Freud's structural hypothesis, the superego is the agency in our psyches related to conscience and morality. The superego is involved with processes such as approval and disapproval of wishes based on their morality, critical self-observation, and a sense of guilt over wrongdoing. The functions of the superego are largely unconscious and are opposed to id elements in our psyches. Mediating between the two and trying to balance them are our egos.

Symbol. Literally speaking, a symbol is something that stands for something else. The term comes from the Greek word symballein, which means "to put together." Advertisers use symbols because they have powerful emotional effects on people. Think, for example, of all that is found in three symbols: the cross, the Star of David, and the crescent. In C.S. Peirce's theory of semiotics, there are three kinds of signs: icons, which communicate by resemblance;

indexes, which communicate by cause and effect; and symbols, whose meaning must be learned. Advertisers make use of symbols because of their power to affect human emotions.

Taste. This term generally is understood to involve people's liking of things, the sense people have that some article of clothing looks good, some kinds of food taste delicious and other areas where choice is a factor and one's choice demonstrates one's attitudes and feelings about something. As Pierre Bourdieu explains in his book *Distinction* (1984:1): "Whereas the ideology of charisma regards taste in legitimate culture as a gift of nature, scientific observation shows that cultural needs are the product of upbringing and education...and preferences in literature, painting, or music, are closely linked to educational level (measured by qualifications or length of schooling) and secondarily to social origin."

Text. For our purposes, a text is, broadly speaking, any work of art in any medium. Critics use the term text as a convenience—so they don't have to name a given work all the time or use various synonyms. There are problems involved in determining what the text is when we deal with serial texts, such as soap operas or comics. In this book, I use the term to stand for literary works, popular culture works, print advertisements, radio and television commercials, and any other kind of advertising or commercial messages carried by any medium.

Theory. I make a distinction between theories and concepts. Theories, as I use the term, are expressed in language and systematically and logically attempt to explain and predict phenomena being studied. They differ from concepts, which define phenomena that are being studied, and from models, which are abstract, usually graphic, and explicit about what is being studied. For example, Freud developed psychoanalytic theory, and one of the concepts in this theory is what he called the unconscious.

Typology. We will understand typology as a system of classification of things used to organize ideas and concepts and enable us to see relationships of interest.

Uses and Gratifications. This sociological theory argues that researchers should pay attention to the way audiences use the media (or certain texts or genres of texts, such as soap operas, print advertisements, or radio and television commercials) and the gratifications they get from their use of these texts and the media. Uses and gratifications researchers focus, then, on how audiences use the media and not on how the media affects audiences.

Values. Values are abstract and general beliefs or judgments about what is right and wrong and what is good and bad that have implications for individual behavior and social, cultural, and political entities. There are some problems with values from a philosophical point of view. First, how does one determine which values are correct and good and which aren't? That is, how do we justify values? Are values objective or subjective? Second, what happens when there is a conflict between groups, each of which holds a central value that conflicts with that of another group?

Warner, W. Lloyd. An anthropologist and sociologist whose work on social class in the United States was of major importance. He elaborated a famous typology that argued that there are six classes in America: upper-upper, lower-upper, upper-middle, lower-middle, upper-lower, and lower-lower, with lower-middle- and upper-lower forming the "common man" (and now common woman) level.

Weber, Max. (1864-1920) A German sociologist, philosopher, and political economist widely regarded as one of the founding figures of modern sociology. He is best known for his work on the sociology of religion, the sociology of bureaucracy, and the concept of social action. Weber's most famous work is his book, *The Protestant Ethic and the Spirit of Capitalism*, in which he argued that the Protestant Reformation and its emphasis on individualism and hard work helped to create the conditions necessary for the rise of capitalism. He also developed the concept of the "ideal type," which is a conceptual model that represents the essential characteristics of a social phenomenon.

Youth Culture. Youth cultures are subcultures formed by young people around some area of interest, usually connected with leisure and entertainment, such as rock music, computer games, hacking, and ways of dressing. These cultures generally develop institutions that cater to their needs.

References

Alfonseca, Kiara. 2022, June 21. "Threats and violence: LGBTQ community faces renewed political battles during Pride Month." *ABC News.* https://abcnews.go.com/U.S./threats-violence-lgbtq-community-faces-renewed-political-battles/story?id=85409645

Aristotle. *Politics.*

Berger, Arthur Asa. 2004. *Ocean Tourism and Cruising.* New York, NY: Haworth.

Blake, Elizabeth. "Single? You're not Alone." *The Conversation.* February 1, 2023 B1.

Blanner, Katherine M. 2016, January 18. "Shakespeare's definition of love." *The Odyssey Online.* https://www.theodysseyonline.com/shakespeares-definition-love

Borges, Jorge Luis. 1941. "The Garden of Forking Paths." https://archive.org/details/TheGardenOfForkingPathsJorgeLuisBorges1941

Bourdieu, Pierre. 1993. *Sociology in Question.* London: Sage Publications.

Brenner, Charles. 1974. *An elementary textbook of psychoanalysis.* Revised and expanded ed. Garden City, NY: Doubleday.

Butler, Judith. 1999. *Gender Trouble: Feminism and the subversion of identity.* New York, NY: Routledge.

Chandler, Daniel. 2002. *Semiotics: The Basics.* New York: Routledge.

Claritas. (n.d.). https://www.claritas.com/, 1-888-981-4 1 888 981 4 CONTACT US

Cohen, Erik. 1972. "Towards a Sociology of International Tourism," *Social Research: An International Quarterly*, 39.

Cortese, Anthony J. 1999. *Provocateur: Images of Women and Minorities in Advertising.* 2nd Edit. Lanham, MD: Roman & Littlefield.

Cruise Line Types. (n. d). *All Things Cruise* https://allthingscruise.com/cruise-line-types-figuring-out-what-the-different-categories-mean/

De Certeau, Michel de. 1988. *The Practice of Everyday Life.* Berkeley, CA: University of California Press.

Dickinson, Bob and Vladimir, Andy. 1997. *Selling the Seas: An Inside Look at the Cruise Industry.* New York: John Wiley.

Emont, Jon. 2023. "Bitter, Scorned Coffee Bean Seeks New Respect from Java Snobs." *The Wall Street Journal.* Feb. 9.

Freud, Sigmund. 1963. *Character and Culture.* New York, NY: Collier Books.

Freud, Sigmund. 1965. *New Introductory Lectures in Psychoanalysis.* New York, NY: W.W. Norton.

Fromm, Erich. 1962. *Beyond the Chains of Illusion: My encounter with Marx and Freud.* New York: Simon & Schuster.

Gottdiener, Mark. 1997. *The Theming of America: Dreams, Visions and Commercial Spaces.* Boulder. CO: Westview.

Greenblatt, Stephen. 2018. *The Norton Anthology of English Literature.* New York, NY: W.W. Norton.

Grucela, Adam. 2023, June 12. "Cruise industry statistics." *Passport Photo Online*. https://passport-photo.online/blog/cruise-industry-statistics

Guzman, Karen. 2023, February 17. "Pursuing work-life balance in a post-pandemic world." *Yale School of Management*. https://som.yale.edu/story/2023/pursuing-work-life-balance-post-pandemic-world

Hackley, Chris. 2013. *Marketing in Context*. London: Springer.

Harvard University Press. (n.d.). Harvard University Press Book Catalog. Retrieved from https://www.hup.harvard.edu/catalog.php?isbn=9780674212770

Hinsie, L.E. & R.J. Campbell. 1970. *Psychiatric Dictionary*. (4th ed.). New York, NY: Oxford University Press.

Holquist, Michael. (Ed.) 1981. *The Dialogic Imagination: Four Essays by M.M. Bakhtin*. Austin, Texas: University of Texas Press.

International Association for Semiotic Studies. (n.d.). "Import of Semiotics in the Study of Brands." *International Journal of Marketing Semiotics*. iass-ais.org/cfp-international-journal-of-marketing-semiotics/

Jones, Jeffrey M. 2023, February 22. "U.S. LGBT Identification Steady at 7.2%." *Gallup*. https://news.gallup.com/poll/470708/lgbt-identification-steady.aspx

King James Bible Online. (n.d.). *Genesis 3:1-19*. King James Bible Online. https://www.kingjamesbibleonline.org/Genesis-Chapter-3/

Klein, Melanie and Joan Riviere. 1964. *Love, Hate and Reparation*. New York: W.W. Norton

Kotler, Philip, John Bowen & James Makens. 1999. *Marketing for Hospitality Tourism*. 2nd Ed. Upper Saddle River, New Jersey: Prentice Hall.

Lakoff, G. and M. Johnson. 1980. *Metaphors We Live By*. Chicago: University of Chicago Press.

Lazere, Donald. 1977. "Mass culture, political consciousness, and English Studies. *College English* (755-756).

Lefebvre, Henri. 1984. *Everyday Life in the Modern World*. New Brunswick, NJ: Transaction.

Library.net. (n.d.). "Grid and group cultural theory and organisational culture." https://1library.net/article/grid-and-group-cultural-theory-organisational-culture.q07w51vz

MacCannell, Dean. 1976. *The Tourist; A New Theory of the Leisure Class*. New York: Schocken Books.

Mandavilli, Appurva. 2022, March 10. "Antibiotics After Sex Cuts Risk of Infections for Some, Studies Show." *The New York Times*.

Marx, Karl. 1964. *Selected Writings in sociology and social philosophy*. (T.B. Bottomore & M. Rubel, Eds.) New York: McGraw-Hill.

New World Encyclopedia. (n.d.). "Choice." https://www.newworldencyclopedia.org/entry/Choice

NHS. (n.d.). "Gender dysphoria." https://www.nhs.uk/conditions/gender-dysphoria/

Oswald, Laura. 2007. "Semiotics and Strategic Brand Management." https://marketingsemiotics.com/wp-content/uploads/2019/04/SEMIOTICBRANDSOswald-copy.pdf

Pines, Maya. Oct. 13, 1982. G1. "How They Know What You Really Mean." *San Francisco Chronicle.*

Plog, Stanley. 2001. "Why Destinations Arise and Fail in Popularity." *Cornell University Hotel and Restaurant Administration Quarterly.* Vol. 43, No. 2.

Rapaille, Clotaire. 2006. *The culture code: an ingenious way to understand why people around the world live and buy as they do.* New York, NY: Broadway books.

Rhodes, Mel. 1961. "An Analysis of Creativity." *Phi Delta Kappa International.*

Rieff, Philip. Ed. 1963. *Sigmund Freud: Character and Culture.* New York, NY: Collier Books.

Safran, J.D., and E. Gardner-Schuster. In *Encyclopedia of Mental Health (Second Edition),* 2016. https://www.sciencedirect.com/topics/neuroscience/psycho analytic-theory

Saussure, Ferdinand de. 1966. *A Course in General Linguistics.* (W. Baskin, Trans.). New York: McGraw-Hill. (Original work published in 1915)

Shevtsova, Maria. 1992. Dialogism in the Novel and Bakhtin's Theory of Culture. *New Literary History,* 23(3), 747-763. https://vdocument.in/dialogism-in-the-novel-and-bakhtins-theory-of-culturepdf.html?page=1

Sigall, Harold. 2017, August 17. "Buyer's remorse." *Psychology Today.* https://www.psychologytoday.com/us/blog/wishful-thoughts/201708/buyer-s-remorse

Stanford Encyclopedia of Philosophy. (n.d.). "Edwards, Jonathan." https://plato.stanford.edu/entries/edwards/

Stanford Encyclopedia of Philosophy. (n.d.). "Social choice theory." https://plato.stanford.edu/entries/social-choice/

Stieg, Cory. 2020, October 27. "Does buying a home make you happier? The psychology of home ownership." *CNBC.* https://www.cnbc.com/2020/10/27/does-buying-a-home-make-you-happier-psychology-of-home-ownership.html

Stritof, Sheri. 2022, March 30. "What is romantic love?" *Verywell Mind.* https://www.verywellmind.com/what-is-romantic-love-2303236

Thompson, Michael, Richard Ellis and Aaron Wildavsky. 1990. *Cultural Theory.* Boulder, CO. Westview.

Timsit, Annabelle. 2023, February 21. "Four-day workweek gains momentum in the UK." *The Washington Post.* https://www.washingtonpost.com/wellness/2023/02/21/four-day-work-week-results-uk/

Tourism Academy. 2021, September 15. "U.S. Tourism Travel Statistics 2020-2021." https://blog.tourismacademy.org/us-tourism-travel-statistics-2020-2021

United Nations World Tourism Organization. (n.d.) "Tourism." https://www.unwto.org/glossary-tourism-terms.

UNWTO. (n.d.). "Glossary of tourism terms." https://www.unwto.org/glossary-tourism-terms

Valtorta, Roberta Rosa and Maria Grazia Monaci. 2023. "When Workers Feel Like Objects: A Field Study on Self-Objectification and Affective Commitment." *Europe Journal of Psychology,* 19(1):15-26.

Williams, Raymond. 1977. *Marxism and Literature.* Oxford, UK: Oxford University Press.

Wollen, Peter. 1969. *Signs and Meaning in the Cinema.* New York: Bloomsbury.

World Population Review. (n.d.). "Divorce rates by country." https://worldpopulation review.com/country-rankings/divorce-rates-by-country

Zaltman, G. 2003. *How Customers Think: Essential Insights into the mind of the market.* Cambridge, MA: Harvard University Business School Press.

About the Author

Various Images of the Author and Seal

Arthur Asa Berger is Professor Emeritus of Broadcast and Electronic Communication Arts at San Francisco State University, where he taught from 1965 to 2003. He graduated in 1954 from the University of Massachusetts, where he majored in literature and philosophy. He received an MA in journalism and creative writing from the University of Iowa in 1956. He was drafted shortly after graduating from Iowa and served in the U.S. Army in the Military District of Washington in Washington, D.C., where he was a feature writer and speechwriter in the District's Public Information Office. He also wrote about high school sports for *The Washington Post* on weekend evenings while in the army.

Berger spent a year touring Europe after he left the Army and then went to the University of Minnesota, where he received a Ph.D. in American Studies in 1965. He wrote his dissertation on the comic strip *Li'l Abner*. In 1963-64, he had a Fulbright Scholarship to Italy and taught at the University of Milan. He spent a year as a visiting professor at the Annenberg School for Communication at The University of Southern California in Los Angeles in 1984, and two months in the fall of 2007 as a visiting professor at the School of Hotel and Tourism at the Hong Kong Polytechnic University. He spent a month lecturing at Jinan University in Guangzhou and ten days at Tsinghua University in Beijing in Spring 2009.

He is the author of over one hundred articles published in the United States and abroad, many book reviews, and more than 90 books on the mass media, popular culture, humor, tourism, and everyday life. Among his books are *Bloom's Morning, The Academic Writer's Toolkit: A User's Manual; Media Analysis Technique; Seeing is Believing: An Introduction to Visual Communication; Ads, Fads and Consumer Culture; The Art of Comedy Writing;* and *Shop 'Til You Drop: Consumer Behavior and American Culture.* Berger is also an artist and has illustrated many of his books.

He has also written several comic academic mysteries such as *Postmortem for a Postmodernist, Mistake in Identity, The Mass Comm Murders: Five Media Theorists Self-Destruct,* and *Durkheim is Dead: Sherlock Holmes is Introduced to Sociological Theory.* His books have been translated into German, Italian, Russian, Arabic, Swedish, Korean, Turkish and Chinese, and he has lectured in more than a dozen countries during his career.

Berger is married, has two children and four grandchildren, and lives in Mill Valley, California. He enjoys traveling and classical music.

He can be reached by e-mail at arthurasaberger@gmail.com.

Index of Names

A

Adam, 63-65
Alfonseca, Kiara, 89
Aristotle, 31, 57
Arrow, Kenneth, 20

B

Bachelor, Bob, xi
Bakhtin, Mikhail, 94, 95, 96, xxxi
Black, Duncan, 20
Blake, Elizabeth, 60, xxix
Blanner, Katherine, 56
Borda, Jean-Charles de, 20
Borges, Juan Luis, 96-97, xxxii
Bottomore, Tom, 7
Bourdieu, Pierre, 21, 22, xxv
Bowen, John, 39
Brenner, Charles, 44, 47, 49
Butler, Judith, 86-87

C

Campbell, Robert J., 48
Chandler, Daniel, 34, 35, 87
Chon, Kaye, 78, 79
Cohen, Erik, 75, xxxi
Condorcet, Nicolas de, 20
Cortese, Anthony, 39

D

Dickinson, Bob, 80
Dietrich, Marlene, 57, xxix
Dodgson, Charles, 20
Douglas, Mary, 2, 3, xxiii
Durkheim, Emile, 28-29

E

Eco, Umberto, 37
Edwards, Jonathan, 3, ix, xxiii
Ellis, Richard, 4
Emerson, Caryl, 95
Emont, Jon, 18
Eppli, Mark, 69
Eve, 63-65

F

Feintzeig, Rachel, 62
Freud, Sigmund, 45, 48, 50, xxvii, xxviii

G

Gallup, George, xxxi
Gardener-Schuster, E., 44
Gottdiener, Mark, 35
Gramsci, Antonio, 10
Grucela, Adam, 77
Guilford, J.P, 90
Guzman, Karen, 62

H

Hackley, Chris, 42, xxvii
Hinsie, Leland, 48
Holquist, Michael, 93

J

Johnson, Mark, 40
Jones, Jeffrey, 86

K

Klein, Melanie, 52, 58, xxix
Kotler, Philip, 39

L

Lakoff, George, 40
Lazere, Donald, 6
Lee, Stan, xiv
Lefebvre, Henri, 8, xxiv

M

MacCannell, Dean, 75, xxxi
Makens, James, 39
Mandavilli, Apoorva, 88
Marx, Karl, 5, 6, 7, 8, 65, 66, 67, xii-xxiv, xxx
Monaci, Maria Grazia, 66, xxx

O

Oswald, Laura R, 41, 42, xxvii

P

Peirce, Charles Sanders, 37, xxvi
Pines, Maya, 37, xxvi
Plato, 31
Plog, Stanley, 76, 77, xxxi

R

Remus, George, xiv
Rhodes, Mel, 90
Riviere, Joan, 52, xxviii

S

Safran, J.D., 44
Saussure, Ferdinand de, 36, xxvi

Schopenhauer, Arthur, xxiii
Sen, Amartya, 20
Shakespeare, William, 56
Sigall, Harold, 51
Steig, Cory, 69
Straus, R. Peter, 62
Stritoff, Sheri, 56

T

Thompson, Michael, 2, 4, 5
Timsit, Annabelle, 68

U

Updike, John, xiv

V

Valtorta, Roberta Rosa, 66, xxx
Vladimir, Andy, 80

W

Weber, Max, 65
Wildavsky, Aaron, 4
Williams, Raymond, 9, 10, xxiv
Wollen, Peter, 35

Z

Zaltman, Gerald, 46, xxviii
Zerubavel, Eviatar, 87

Index of Topics

A

"An Analysis of Creativity," 90
An Elementary Textbook of
  Psychoanalysis: Revised and
  Expanded Edition, 44, 47

B

"Bitter, Scorned Coffee Bean Seeks
  New Respect from Java Snobs,"
  18

C

Choices
  and id, ego and superego, xxviii
  Aristotle on, 31
  automobiles, 30
  career to pursue, xv
  choice differs from taste, xxv
  education, 30
  everyday life, 32
  home and location, 30
  how to spend free time, xv
  id, ego and superego, 49-50
  life-changing, xvi
  marriage, 29
  never-ending need to make, xv
  occupations, 29
  political affiliations, 31
  religion, 30-31
  unimportant choices, xvi
  what to eat, xv
  what to wear, xv
  where to live, xv
Choosing a Partner

Aristotle on man is a social
  animal, 57
divorce in the USA, 58-60
Marlene Dietrich on falling in
  love, 57
solo life as better, 60
Civilization and Its Discontents,
  48
Claritas
  Birds of a feather flock together,
  25
  typology, xxvi
  zip codes, 26
Coda
  Bakhtin and dialogic theory,
  95-96
  Borges on choices, 96
  brainstorming on book, 94
  journal 106 and choices book,
  91-93
  labyrinths and choices, 96
  Le Mot Juste, 94

D

Dialogic theory
  Bakhtin on, xxxi
  Intertextuality, 96
  two-way aspects of
  communication, 93
"Does buying a home make you
  happier? The psychology of
  home ownership," 69

E

Education and Work, 63

Encyclopedia of Mental Health
  (Second Edition), 44
Espresso Machine Aficionados
    BonsenKitchen, 8001, 11
    coffee grinders, 14-16
    cost of machines and grinders,
      12-17
    "God shot," and, 13
    my various coffee makers, 12
    number of brands of espressos
      enormous, 12
    types of espresso machines,
      14-15
European Journal of Psychology,
  66
Everyday Life in the Modern
  World, 9

G

Gender Trouble, 86
Genesis 3:1-19, 64
Grid group theory
    binding restrictions and, 4
    four lifestyles, 3-5
    group boundaries and, 2
    Mary Douglas and, xxiii

H

"Hate, Greed and Aggression," 52
Home Espresso Machine
  Aficionados, xxiv
Housing
    finding a house an ordeal, 70
    high cost and homeless, 73
    making changes in, 73
    moving to suburbs for good
      schools, 70
    need to keep repairing homes,
      72

How Customers Think: Essential
  Insights into the Mind of the
  Market, 46
Human freedom
    Arthur Schopenhauer on, xxiii
    Jonathan Edwards on, xxiii

I

International Journal of Marketing
  Semiotics, 34

J

"John Updike: American Writer,
  American Life," xiv

L

LGBTQIA+
    attacks on LGBTQIA+
      community, 88-89
    binarism and, 87-88
    choices possible, 85-86
    diseases and, 88
    Gallup Poll and, 85, xxxi
    gender as a performance, 86-
      87
    gender dysphoria, 84
    Male-Female Binary
      Oppositions chart, 88
    Republicans and, 88
Love, Hate and Reparation, 52, 58

M

Marin Independent Journal, 60
Marketing for Hospitality Tourism,
  39
Marketing in Context: Setting the
  Scene, 42
Marriage

average length of, xxix
cultural universal, xxix
divorce statistics, 59
Marxism
alienation of workers from
selves, 65-66
and choice, xxiii
and contemporary culture, 6
creation of consumer cultures,
8
hegemony, xxiv
ideas of ruling classes
dominant, 7-8
Lefebvre on capitalism and
terror, 8-9
Raymond Williams on
hegemony, 10
ruling classes role, xxiv
work and alienation, xxx
Marxism and Literature, 10
"Mass culture, political
consciousness and English
Studies," 6

N

New Introductory Lectures on
Psychoanalysis, 48

O

Ocean Cruising Tourism
Erik Cohen typology, 75-76
growth of ocean cruising
industry, 77-78
luxury cruising, 79-81
psychoanalytic perspectives
on, 82-83
report on Princess Cruise, 81-
82
Stanley Plog typology, 76-77
Ocean Tourism and Cruising, 79

"One of the Difficulties of
Psychoanalysis," 45

P

Phi Delta Kappa International, 90
Politics, 57
Provocateur: Images of Women
and Minorities in Advertising,
39
Psychoanalysis
Brenner on id, ego and
superego, 47-48
buyer's remorse, 51-52
defense mechanisms, 50-51
Freud on the id, 48
Freud on three levels of
consciousness, 45-46
Freud's 'structural' hypothesis,
47
greed and being worthy of love,
53
id, ego, superego and culture,
50
id, ego and superego defined,
44
theory, 44
United Airlines Advertisement,
48-49
Zaltman on human mind, 46-
47
Psychology Today, 51
"Pursuing work-life balance in a
post-pandemic World," 62

R

Roadhouse Blues: Morrison, the
Doors, and the Death Days of
the Sixties. xiv

S

Semiotics
    analysis of Fidji advertisement,
      40-41
    and study of brands, 34
    branding defined, 42
    brands and the self, xxvii
    brands defined, 39
    linguistic devices and
      branding, 39-40
    Maya Pines on signs as
      messages, 37
    metaphor and metonymy, 39-
      40
    Peirce on icons, indexes and
      symbols, 37-38
    Saussure on signs, 36
    science of signs, xxvi
    sending and receiving
      messages, xxvi
    signs defined, 35
    Umberto Eco on aberrant
      decoding, 37
"Semiotics and Strategic Brand
  Management," 41
Semiotics: The Basics First
  Edition, 34
Semiotics: The Basics Third
  Edition, 87
"Shakespeare's definition of
  Love," 56
Signs and Meaning in the Cinema,
  35
Social Choice Theory
    defined, 20
    scholars associated with, 20
Sociology of Choice
    Case study: morning breakfast
      routine, 23-24
    choosing a home, 24-25
    Claritas typology, 25-28

    Emile Durkheim's theories, 28-
      29
    Pierre Bourdieu and taste, 21-
      22
    taste versus choice, 21
Stan Lee: The Man Behind Marvel,
  xiv

T

"Tales of the Bourbon King: The
  Life and True Crimes of George
  Remus," xiv
"The Garden of Forking Paths," 96
The Tourist: A New Theory of the
  Leisure Class, 75
"Threats and Violence: LGBTQ
  community faces renewed
  political battles during Pride
  Month," 89
Tourism: Principles, Practices,
  Philosophes. Eighth edition. 75
Tourism
    defined, xxxi
    kinds of, xxxi
    statistics on, 74
"Toward a Sociology of
  International Tourism," 75

U

"U.S. LGBT identification Steady
  at 7.2%," 86
U.S. Tourism Travel Statistics 2020-
  2021, 74
United Nations World Tourism
  Organization, 75
University of California, Berkeley,
  69

W

"What is Romantic Love?" 56

"When Workers Feel Like Objects: A Field Study on Self-Objectification and Affective Organizational Commitment," 66

Work

    Adam and Eve story in Bible and, 63-64

    educational level and, 63

    impact of Covid-19 pandemic, 67-68

9 781648 897962